A RETURN TO CIVILITY AND A PATH TO GET THERE

"We need this book in a time which civility, responsibility, accountability, and compassion have become unfashionable. David Medeiros has a huge heart, and he helps us understand with his wisdom and humility how it got that way. Better still, he helps us understand how the Internal Family Systems model of therapy can help us all take joy in healing ourselves and our relationships."

—Michael Elkin, LMFT, Senior Trainer in IFS
and author of Families Under the Influence

"As a theater and dance center that works with many young people who have experienced trauma, we had a wish to know someone like David Medeiros—someone with his credentials and skill set, someone with his generosity, someone who would recognize our common ground and our common humanity. Since he began working with us almost ten years ago, he has saved many young people's lives. This book is a reflection of his influences and integration of models of psychotherapy, the performance arts, real-life experiences, and relevance of universal truths.

"He has endlessly used his creativity and expertise to make life easier for so many of our youth who suffer from trauma. At Everett, we often count on our ability to manifest that wish. We did just that with David."

—Dorothy & Aaron Jungels, Co-Founding
Artistic Directors, Everett: Company, Stage & School

"David Medeiros' honor and respect for the dignity of us all as we wade through the human condition radiates through sharing his own journey in A Return to Civility and a Path to Get There. David graciously invites us on a call to grow up and become who we really are for ourselves and the world. It's timely, timeless, and about time."

—Dan Reed, Ph.D., LPC, BCN

A Return to Civility and a Path to Get There

An Exploration of Responsibility, Accountability, and Compassion

DAVID MEDEIROS

A Return to Civility and a Path to Get There:
An Exploration of Responsibility, Accountability,
and Compassion
Copyright © 2020 David Medeiros

Produced and printed
by Stillwater River Publications.
All rights reserved. Written and produced in the
United States of America. This book may not be reproduced
or sold in any form without the expressed, written
permission of the author and publisher.

Visit our website at
www.StillwaterPress.com
for more information.

First Stillwater River Publications Edition

ISBN: 978-1-952521-56-0

Library of Congress Control Number: 2020920490

1 2 3 4 5 6 7 8 9 10
Written by David Medeiros
Published by Stillwater River Publications,
Pawtucket, RI, USA.

TEXT SET IN CRIMSON.

Publisher's Cataloging-In-Publication Data
(Prepared by The Donohue Group, Inc.)

Names: Medeiros, David, 1955- author.
Title: A return to civility and a path to get there : an exploration of
responsibility, accountability, and compassion / David Medeiros.
Description: First Stillwater River Publications edition. |
Pawtucket, RI, USA : Stillwater River Publications, [2020]

Identifiers: ISBN 9781952521560

Subjects: LCSH: Social values--United States--History--21st century. |
Courtesy--United States--History--21st century. |
Interpersonal relations--United States--History--21st century. |
Responsibility--United States--History--21st century. |
United States--Social conditions--21st century.
Classification: LCC BJ1533.C9 M44 2020 | DDC 177.1--dc23

The views and opinions expressed
in this book are solely those of the author
and do not necessarily reflect the views
and opinions of the publisher.

This book is dedicated to all the teachers and mentors who have given so much and generously shared their presence, time, and expertise. To my father-in-law, Al Colella, for helping plant the seed to write this book. And to my partner and wife, Tricia, and our three treasures: Samantha (Sammy, Samurai), Emily (Butterfly of Light), and Christina (My Paco). I could have never done this without you. I love you all!

CONTENTS

Acknowledgments .... *ix*
Introduction .... *xiii*

PART 1: THE BASICS
1. Definitions of Foundational Terms and Concepts 1
2. Universal Truths 8

PART 2: MY PATHS TO UNIVERSAL TRUTHS
3. "It's for Use"—The Tai Chi Story 15
4. Practical Use and Applications of Tai Chi Chuan 20
5. The Drum Masters 23

PART 3: THE PSYCHOLOGICAL UNDERPINNINGS
6. Overview of the Internal Family System Model 33
7. Cognitive Physio Mechanisms 46
8. Interview with Richard Schwartz, PhD 51

PART 4: THE REAL WORLD
9. Opportunities Lost 61

PART 5: CAUTIONARY TALES
10. What Can Erode a Sense of Responsibility,
    Accountability, and Civility? 79

PART 6: THE FUTURE
11. Hope & The Principle of Responsibility and
    Civility Redefined 105
12. Lofty Goals 125
Conclusion 131

APPENDIX A: Cognitive Physio Mechanisms (CPM) *137*
APPENDIX B: Interviews with Ann Sinko, LMFT;
   Rina Dubin, Ed.D.; and Michael Elkin, LMFT *141*
APPENDIX C: Education and Leadership *179*
Bibliography *182*
Photography Credits *188*

ACKNOWLEDGMENTS

The "seed" for this book was significantly influenced by my father-in-law, Al Colella. Many years ago, I was the co-director of an agency which conducted Domestic Violence/Abuse Psychoeducational groups for men who had been arrested and convicted for domestic violence/abuse. One morning, I was having breakfast with Al, and I was discussing how difficult it could be to talk about responsibility in these groups. I was trying to develop a concept of responsibility that could serve as some type of foundation and framework. It was clear to me there was something reinforcing to these men that they experienced when they would be abusive. It was also clear that some agencies would try to shame the men into being respectful to women. That did not work at all. It was Al who suggested the term "Principle of" as a way to establish a type of standard, much like there are theorems and laws in mathematics or the sciences. Given Al earned a Ph.D. in mathematics and electrical engineering, I was more than willing to take his word for it. During our breakfast, we wrote the term "The Principle of Responsibility" out on a napkin and I wrote the definition as: knowing the difference between right and wrong. Unfortunately, I lost that napkin, but I did not lose the memory and inspiration that helped plant the seed to write this book many years later. Thank you Al/Dad! I want to thank Anthony Testa, Ph.D., my first true mentor at CCRI; Lt. Col. Phillip Gilchrist for his valuable and real life insights into the experience and cost of war.

Ron Schertz, Ph.D. Ron helped guide this guy who didn't have a clue about college, and he really was a sherpa leading me through the maze of beginning college at almost thirty years old. Classes, professors, basic instruction, financial aid, and a hefty amount of gut busting laughter were all aspects of Dr. (Ron) Schertz's influence and help. E. Bel Evans, Ph.D., my teacher and mentor for 2 years and for sharing her incredible wealth of knowledge, and suggesting if I was going to be a therapist, it would really help if I undertook the process as a client as well. Franicis Pescosolido, Ph.D., treasured teacher, mentor, and friend; All of my IFS Level I training compadres including: The Fabulous Women of Texas, Julie Aresco, Hugh O'Doherty, Joan Trainer, Richard Magnon, Jennie Knott, Leslie Maurer, Leela Howard, Deborah Jacobs, and Laura Kottkamp. Ginger Phakos, PA and friend extraordinaire. I want to thank John Peters, therapist, PA, and comedian with laser precise timing, and the first person to suggest I could be a PA. Ellis Waldman. I have had the privilege to provide consultation to and for Ellis Waldman, CEO of Walco Electronics. He is one of the most honorable human beings I know, and on the top tier of my personal and professional respect. He has kept his company afloat (and that means preserving his employees' jobs) during economic downturns, rescissions, embezzlement, and now COVID. Thank you Captain, it's been an honor to serve on your ship. Joanna Friedlander and Anne Farley Cremer—for your support and laughs in Chicago! Michael Cumerford, (Mr. D.) D. J. wouldn't be here without you buddy! Tia Priolo, JD—practices the profession of law honorably. To the entire Green Hill beach gang. Drummers such as: Clyde Stubblefield and John "Jabo" Starks, pioneers of funk; Benny Benjamin and the Funk Brothers; Al Jackson, Jr. and Booker T. & the MGs; Elvin Jones; Roger Hawkins of the Muscle Shoals Rhythm Section; Harvey Mason, David Garibaldi and TOP—RIP Francis Rocco Prestia; Keith Carlock, and Buddy Williams -and thank you for your advice!—and many more. Adele Laurie Blue—I thought it might be Ash Sloan—kudos to you, playing drums on Hello. Well done! Owen "DRENT" Lefebvre, rapper who covers IFS, EMDR, and *The Body Keeps the Score*. Virginia Magnan, treasured friend, former bandmate (what a *voice*), and Clinical Nurse Manager at Hospice who pays it forward at such an important time. Andy Nowak, my goal in life is to make you lose consciousness from laughing so hard. To N.P. for being N.P. Debra Siegel, Ph.D.—your teaching and the gift of the generalist perspective. Ashley Curley, Conference Manager for the IFS Institute and National Conferences who, with her team, pays it forward in so many ways, and was so instrumental in finding a way for Everett and

Acknowledgments

Good Grief to come to Colorado. Thank you Ashley. Jim Carey, I will find a way for the piece I wrote for this book on you, your acting journey, and *Liar Liar* to see the light of day someway-somehow! Sigrid Kulkowitz, MA, MFT—you're in! Thank you to Steven and Dawn Porter and Emma St. Jean at Stillwater River Publications (and Stephen King's *On Writing*) for helping me through the process of becoming a first-time author. Suzanne Borstein, Ph.D., author of *Adjunctive EMDR* and treasured friend, teacher, and mentor. Melisa Verrecchia, thank you for your willingness to have your video shown. Lori Mason-Dalessio, my grammar and writing coach. With me every step of the way! We did it! And to Ann Colella, (Ma Ma) we're a *family*, and I am forever grateful.

INTRODUCTION

The Seed

Sometimes a life-changing idea starts as a tiny seed, planted in the most unlikely of places. I was playing drums in the band Naked Truth, which was later renamed Steve Smith and The Nakeds. It was in the mid 1980's, and we had a gig at The Casino by the Sea, a famous nightclub in Cape Cod, Massachusetts. The Casino was everything you could imagine in a vacation destination; it was located right on the beach and, to put it *mildly*, was a wild place. Stories from those days are still told by musicians and club-goers from all over the country who came through the Casino in its heyday. During that time, we often performed with John Cafferty and the Beaver Brown Band. Beaver Brown was beginning to ride the crest of fame that went with their recording the soundtrack album for the movie *Eddie and the Cruisers*. While the movie initially faltered, the soundtrack began to gather traction based on the strength of the music, and eventually sold over three million albums. The drummer, Kenny Jo Silva (that's a great rock and roll name, by the way) and I were hanging out, and we started talking about drums—practice concepts, keeping time, and recording. Kenny Jo was a powerhouse on drums and possessed a great sense of time.

Time: for a drummer, it is one of our most important responsibilities. One critical aspect of time is the ability to count off a song at the right tempo and maintain that "speed" throughout the song. Kenny Jo talked about how he was taking lessons in Boston with a teacher named Gary Chaffee. Mr. Chaffee was the chair of the Percussion Department at Berklee College of Music. One of the things Kenny was working on was his sense of time. Kenny talked about Mr. Chaffee's concepts about creating "time feels," breaking down beats into different increments (for example eighth, 16th, or triplets), independence, and ultimately developing an even more solid sense of time. He explained that playing with a "good time feel" enables a musician to eventually play or "fiddle" with the time and create different effects and textures.

I was shocked when Kenny Jo told me he was working on this aspect of his playing! As we musicians say, his time was "solid as a rock." This was a touchy spot for me because of how I struggled with my sense of time and meter. It was not unusual for me to speed up or slow down during a song, and some nights my time was better than others. I often practiced three to five hours a day, but over the course of years could not and did not make significant improvement in this aspect of my drumming. Kenny Jo, understanding the difficulty I had in this area, suggested I look into lessons as well. He could arrange the introduction and felt confident Mr. Chaffee would consider taking me on as a student. I remember my answer as if it were yesterday: "I think I'm gonna work on it on my own. Maybe, once I'm better at it, I might give it a try." That answer seems so absurd to me now! Kenny Jo, to his credit, tried again and said he was confident it could really help me, and he emphasized that he could put in a good word to Mr. Chaffee on my behalf. My response and resistance was unshaken. After I dismissed several more attempts, I remember Kenny's eyes drifting off (I do not blame him at all) because he realized there was no getting through to me. Looking back at that time, I realize I had this idea (or a *part* of me did) that I had to do things by myself, and depending on help that might never materialize was a sign of weakness.

Well, not surprisingly, I continued to practice by myself with my own methods, and for the rest of my drumming career I consistently struggled with this critical aspect of being a drummer. It was even worse when we were recording our own album and my stagemanship did not translate to studio musicianship. Eventually I was able to put together some good drum tracks, but it was a very difficult process, actually kind of torturous for me. It was no fun for my band-mates either. We recorded, traveled and toured, and had a small degree of fame. But there was always a

Introduction

level of struggle for me because I never fully addressed this foundational aspect of my musicianship. But, that doesn't mean I didn't learn something very important—actually, life-changing. I didn't realize it during that conversation with Kenny Jo, but the seed had been planted.

The Seed

The life-changing seed which was planted was the concept of responsibility. After I left the band, I began to realize my resistance and refusal to get help with my time keeping had really been incredibly unproductive for me and my bandmates. I began to get curious about *why* I would be so resistant to accepting help for this deficit in my playing. I knew I didn't want to repeat this pattern for the rest of my life. So I decided to begin to look inward and question my motivation for doing something, or not, and to become more responsible and answerable for my choices. I knew there was some type of lesson to be learned from the challenges of my music career—something more, a life template of sorts, that vastly transcended my life as a musician. Later, I learned there was a name that encapsulated these types of experiences. They were called universal truths.

A universal truth is something which is self evident and exists whether we believe it or not. You may debate what gravity is in a philosophical and/or existential discussion, but jump out a second story window and there will be little doubt as to its existence. Less physically tangible, but every bit as important and true are the universal truths such as the Principles of Dignity and Respect, and the driving value behind the idiom "Do unto others as you would have them do unto you." Versions of these universal truths are echoed in almost all cultures, religions, and countries. From the beginning of recorded time, universal truths such as compassion, empathy, and love have been opposed by the universal truths of prejudice, oppression, and fear. They are the yin and yang of our world.

I propose that responsibility is also a universal truth. Its essence is infused into all other universal truths, and is the foundation of this book. Without it, principles and idioms are easily distorted and paradoxically, can be utilized to subjugate and oppress. For instance, a person may embrace "Do unto others..." as long as the "others" are of the same color, culture, religion, socioeconomic status, etc. And if not, the "other" can become "less than" and therefore a supposedly "universal" truth can become contextualized so it longer applies *to those people.* Historically, our own Declaration of Independence clearly illustrates this point in the passage, "We hold these truths to be self evident", and "that all men are created equal." This historic document identified that universal truths exist, and yet at the same time, it codified the systemic oppression of women and the defilement of African males, females, and children who were kidnapped, enslaved, tortured, murdered, not considered human, and sold as property.

With the benefit of a historical perspective, as well as present day, we will explore the incredibly important critical role responsibility, accountability, and civility serve in our everyday lives. Together we will look at one proposed path, named the Internal Family Systems Model, to more fully embody these universal truths, with the understanding there are many paths to reclaim these foundational aspects of being a human being. However, while there can be different paths, the destination remains the same. How can we as a nation collectively embody responsibility, accountability, and civility? At this time in our country's history, all three are under assault. It's time for a call to action.

PART 1

THE BASICS

As the regal Maya Angelou has said,
"Words are things, I'm convinced.
Words are things, you must be careful,
careful about calling people out of their names,
using racial pejoratives, and sexual pejoratives,
and all that ignorance. Don't do that.
Someday we will be able to measure the power of words.
I think they are things, I think they get on the walls,
they get on your wallpaper, they get in your drugs,
in your upholstery, in your clothes,
and finally into you."
—*Oprah Winfrey, Oprah's Master Class interview*

Maya Angelou at the Clinton inauguration

CHAPTER 1

DEFINITIONS OF FOUNDATIONAL TERMS AND CONCEPTS

I love researching words and believe they hold incredible importance. Because words play such an influential role in the way human beings communicate, I am often on a quest, investigating any resources available to me, to understand their nuances, meaning, and power.

In this chapter, I have provided definitions of the terms, words, and concepts that are integrated throughout this book so that you, the reader, are aware of exactly how I am using them. These definitions establish the foundation and framework of this book. Though these are terms and concepts we use a lot in everyday life and we may deem them to be self-evident, it's surprising how often a gap exists between one person's understanding and another's. And in that gap is where things start to break down. There also can be a gap between theory and practice, so I have included scenarios below to illustrate the words, terms, and concepts in real-life situations.

Foundational Terms and Concepts

Civil: Refraining from rudeness or being polite in a perfunctory way. (This is the most rudimentary definition of *civil* and represents the minimum requirement to meet the standard. We will explore this concept later in this book.)

Responsibility: The ability to choose for oneself between right and wrong. To be accountable.

Accountable: The concept of being answerable.

Internal Accountability: When one's decision-making process is governed by a process within themselves, i.e. "I will do it because it's the right thing to do".

External Accountability: When one's decision-making process is governed by a process outside themselves, i.e. a law, a cultural expectation, a religion, etc.

The Principle of Responsibility: The point at which we accept accountability for our thoughts, choices, and actions. The contextual framework of when and how we make decisions can influence the moral meaning we attach to them.

Respect: Consideration for.

Dignity: Inherent nobility and worth.

Ethics: Moral principles, rules of conduct, values.

Morals: Founded on fundamental principles and universal truths of conduct rather than on legalities.

Integrity: Adherence to moral and ethical principles, soundness of moral character, honesty.

Inherent: Existing in someone or something as a permanent and inseparable element, quality, or attribute.

These terms, without a practical application to our daily lives, would be of little value. Therefore, a theme of this book is: how do we put these terms and principles into action? Where do we see them in the real world? Let me begin with a couple of little stories I often tell in my office.

Scenario One:

You are driving your car late at night and find yourself stopped at a red light. You are waiting for it to change. There is not a single car, bus, or motorcycle anywhere in sight. You are becoming increasingly frustrated, waiting at this light without seeing a single car on the road. You inch forward a bit, look around, and even wonder if the light is broken. You decide to run the red light but then pause to just think for a moment. Is it really the safest thing to run the red light? "Something could happen, even though it seems unlikely," you think. "And even if someone comes speeding down the road with their lights off and we crash, I'm still responsible to some degree. That wouldn't be right, so I'll just wait." The light finally changes and you are on your way.

Scenario Two:

Here is the same basic scenario, but in this version, you decide to inch through the light and realize there is a police officer just off to the side with their lights off. You hit the brakes and hope you haven't gone too far through the intersection to get a ticket. You hold your breath as your eyes shift to the side, praying not to see that ominous flash of red. The light changes. As you continue to drive away you try to look inconspicuous, and keep peeking at the rearview mirror to see if the police officer is following you.

Scenario Three:

Same basic scenario at the traffic light. You go through the process of what's the "right" choice to make in this situation, you look around carefully once more, no cars are coming, there are no police cars in sight, and you slowly cruise through the red traffic light. Once past the light you continue on your way with the knowledge there was no accident, no harm, no police, no ticket, no foul.

Scenario Four:

A similar scenario at the traffic light, but this time your child is in the car because they woke up with a 106 fever; they are in Ketoacidosis (which can be a life threatening diabetic condition), and you are rushing them to the hospital in the middle of the night. You are definitely speeding, though not recklessly. As you pull up to the red light, you quickly look around, see no cars, and you shoot through the light, definitely breaking the speed limit, and bring your child to the hospital where they are treated successfully.

Scenario Five:

Same basic situation as Scenario Four, but this time you are driving really recklessly. You see the traffic light; maybe it's even yellow, and you gun the engine even faster, flying through the red light, and suddenly see a car coming (legally) through the intersection. You T-bone the other car going about 60 mph. Bad things ensue...

So let's look at each pretty straightforward scenario briefly and explore how they fit into responsibility and accountability.

Scenario One (You waited): This is an example of Internal Accountability. The locus of control, logic, and ultimate decision making is coming from an internal source. In addition, in the context of the greater good, it makes sense.

Scenario Two (You inched forward): This is an example of External Accountability. The locus of control, logic, and ultimate decision making is coming from an external source: the police officer and the consequences of running a red light, being stopped, getting a ticket, etc.

Scenario Three (You went for it): This is an example of grappling with both internal and external aspects of accountability and making the "less" responsible choice.

Scenario Four (You had a sick child!): When I pose this example most parents say: "That's what I would do," with no guilt or regrets. I ask you, the reader, to ponder this scenario and consider whether it sounds like a "responsible" course of action.

Scenario Five (You had a sick child, so you gunned it.): This scenario can result in harm, injury, maiming, or death, and it clearly does not align with the Principle of Responsibility. However, who would argue the driver wasn't trying to do something good: to save their child? I call it, "Doing the 'right' thing in the 'wrong' way."

Most of us have done something like the first four of these scenarios. I sure have! And I have also done the fifth scenario without the result of injuring or killing others. I am not proud of it, but it is true.

Scenario Five poses an interesting quandary about responsibility, accountability, and choice—and also exposes a major challenge of advocating for a return to civility via responsibility. Is the Principle of Responsibility this rigid, black and white, moralistic model? Is the opposite of being responsible being irresponsible? Is the opposite of dignity, degradation? Is Internal Accountability more valuable than External Accountability? It would be wonderful if all these questions could be answered in a black and white, definitive way—but that's not real life. However, it can be useful to think in absolutes because they bring certain questions to the surface that we all should be asking ourselves if we are interested in setting a course for responsibility and civility. It can be a difficult process.

I have made my share, and more, of mistakes and had moments, hours, days, and significant periods of behaving irresponsibly. I can assure you it is not my intention to present myself in this book as someone who always knows what the right choice is, and makes it. What this book hopes to illuminate, is that we each have the power to carve and tend to our own self-led path. Furthermore, if we find that we have drifted down an unexpected, unhealthy, or unproductive trail (that is incongruent to our sense of self), we can learn to understand how we got there. If we can remain curious and compassionate towards ourselves and others, we have a much better chance to formulate a plan and find the compass that will reset our course. You already have that power and force in you.

Although these traffic examples may seem simplistic, being responsible in the decision making process often is that straightforward. This in no way infers that being responsible and internally accountable is this black and white formula. In fact, these concepts can lead to quandaries that can be quite challenging (even painful) and can require us to examine our preconceived beliefs. However, as will be demonstrated in Chapter 9, human beings (even presidents of the United States) have abdicated (at times) the simple principles behind the stories of the traffic light. How do we know this? Well, to be blunt, it usually doesn't take a rocket scientist (or someone with that level of intellect and education) to figure out how to do the right thing.

However, in some situations a rocket scientist is required. In fact, I am very fortunate to have such a person just a phone call away. Dr. Rick

Reamer, my former Professor in the graduate program of the School of Social Work, at Rhode Island College, has chaired the committee to write the National Association of Social Workers' (NASW) Code of Ethics, which is also the standard world-wide for our profession, and has traveled around the globe teaching ethics.

I have utilized Dr. Reamer's formidable skills in several situations. Sometimes figuring out what is ethical can be challenging and requires significant research. And it takes on an extra level of complexity when you are in the position of a social worker, and someone has come to you looking for help with this very issue. For example, let's say I am seeing a client who decides to do something that could lead to potential risk or harm (though not physical) to themselves or others. At that juncture, I would be responsible to have reviewed our Code of Ethics, cite the specific sections involved, conceptualize mitigating circumstances, share these concerns with the client, provide thorough documentation of the entire process, and seek consultation with an expert in the field. During this involved process, I am very lucky to be able to consult with Dr. Reamer. In this instance, my responsibility would be to inform the client of my concerns, potential consequences, and risks. But ultimately, how to act is the client's decision, something that is supported by the standard of Self Determination in the NASW Code of Ethics.

However, many ethical, responsibility, and accountability issues can be answered with a question I have heard Dr. Reamer repeat numerous times. He puts it quite succinctly: "The question to ask ourselves is: 'What would a *reasonable* social worker do in the same situation?'" This question, with one change, could also be a template for anyone when considering responsibility and accountability: "What would a *reasonable person* do in the same situation?"

So our next challenge is how we would define *reasonable*. Reasonable can be defined as having sound judgement and rational behavior. However, what is *reasonable* for one person or group may be completely *unreasonable* for another person or group. Take, for example, the oppression of women or the institution of racism. These, and several more *isms*, can be presented as "reasonable," as long as you're not part of the oppressed group. This paradigm is particularly intriguing to me, given I am pos-

Definitions of Foundational Terms and Concepts

tulating that the principles in this book, at times, cannot be reduced to a rigid black-or-white, either/or, right-wrong examination. Explorations into what is considered reasonable in our personal life, profession, culture, etc. often require us to investigate the contextual framework including what we are taught, what culture we are from, what culture we live in, and what influences and experiences have shaped what we *believe* as universal truths. However, exploring the contextual framework is not an excuse, in any way, for oppression and darkness. *In fact, I have an absolute conviction there are basic foundational underpinnings of moral and universal truths.*

I also have an absolute conviction we all make mistakes and irresponsible choices. It's part of being a human being. So it's absolutely necessary we have a model to explore our imperfectness with curiosity and compassion, have the courage to question our beliefs, and eagerly (or maybe kicking and screaming) be willing to explore our roots and origins.

Lastly, an all-too-familiar scenario involves those individuals or groups who know the difference between right and wrong, but make the conscious decision to do the latter *anyway*. Furthermore, when the proverbial poop hits the fan, the people who have made irresponsible choices usually bring others down with them. These elements will be reviewed in Chapter 9 as well.

> **TO CONSIDER:** What are your universal truths? What do you believe about the world and yourself that is "automatic" to your understanding of human nature that you consider to be self-evident? What "truths" might be influenced by gender, race, family, culture, the time period you live in, or religious and economic status?

CHAPTER 2

UNIVERSAL TRUTHS

In the late '80's, approaching thirty years of age, I changed my primary focus from being a musician to pursuing an Associates Degree in Liberal Arts at the Community College of Rhode Island (CCRI). I still made my living playing music, but began a transition from drums to playing guitar and singing. It was there at CCRI that I was lucky enough to meet my first true mentor, Professor Anthony Testa. He was teaching *Introduction to Psychology*, and through fate or luck, I chose his class as a general education requirement. Professor Testa was a wonderful teacher, with a passion for the subject matter. I distinctly remember sitting in his class and having the "light bulb" go off in my head when I felt the same kind of spark for psychology as I did for music. Professor Testa recognized my initial passion and was incredibly instrumental in shepherding me through the substantial challenges of having played in a band for twelve years really having no academic skills to speak of, and lighting the intellectual fire that still burns thirty-five years later.

This is when the seed that was planted during that conversation with Kenny Jo first started to grow. I made a promise to myself at CCRI: if I continued to pursue a career in psychology, I would do it differently than my drumming. I would do my best to take responsibility by listening to feedback from others, utilizing the most effective teachers and professors I could find, and establishing a solid foundation of psychological principles. I wasn't going into this with a weak sense of "time." This decision was a turning point in my life. I am not saying I did not, nor currently do not, experience challenges. Rather, I don't experience them due to the lack of a solid foundational base in psychology. I have always had a teacher and mentor in some vein of psychology since I started as a therapist. I am confident this is not an aspect of overcompensating for the past—rather, it is because I truly love learning and being around people who are willing to share their expertise. After graduating from CCRI, I then enrolled at the University of Rhode Island.

I first learned about the concept of universal truths in a philosophy class at the University of Rhode Island (URI). Our professor defined a universal truth as something that is self-evident, even if we do not believe in its existence. In a philosophy class you may debate in an existential discussion, that gravity is an artificial construct. As I wrote previously, if you jump out of a second story window, the existence of gravity will be apparent—especially on the landing. This example is an observable and consistent universal truth in the physical world, while concepts such as dignity, respect, and "Do unto to others", become more nuanced. However, the idea that we *all deserve* to be treated with dignity and respect *is* a universal truth.

Virtually all cultures and religions contain and value certain universal truths. In particular, some version of the concepts of dignity and respect, and the mantra "Do unto others as you would have them do unto you", is almost always present. Unfortunately, as we'll see in Chapters 7 and 9, it is deceptively simple to circumvent a universal truth in order to conveniently validate how we treat other human beings with a lack of dignity and respect. This leads me to another universal truth that is equally true and serves to show that not all universal truths lead to positive places.

Throughout history, there have been people (groups, cultures, countries, religions) who look to oppress, objectify and subjugate fellow human beings. It is a universal truth that human beings have demonstrated a "willingness to harm." When people profess to me that "everyone is good" in my clinical practice, I need to delve into what they mean by that, because there are infinite examples to the contrary. While a more thorough exploration would include how both men and women are capable of harm, if we are going to be honest, it is a universal truth that men largely own this dubious distinction.

Gavin de Becker, in his book *THE GIFT OF FEAR AND OTHER SIGNALS THAT PROTECT US FROM VIOLENCE*, puts it succinctly and directly:

> *"Men of all ages and in all parts of the world are more violent than women. For this reason, the language in this book is mostly gender-specific to men. When it comes to violence, women can proudly relinquish recognition in the language, because here at least, politically correct would be statistically incorrect."*

Based on historical and empirical evidence, and a lifetime of practical experience, de Becker is absolutely clear in his assessment that men have demonstrated a greater capacity and frequency for violence, as compared to women, throughout the ages. (I have thought for many years that if women governed the world there would be much fewer wars, because I believe women would be much less likely to send their sons, daughters, loved ones, or other human beings into harm's way, unless no other option existed.)

Lastly, the willingness to harm is not black-and-white. During Gavin de Becker's Threat Assessment and Risk Academy, Lt. Col. Dave Grossman (an expert on Killology and lethal force) presented a compelling theory based on a thorough, multi-faceted analysis, that a significant number of soldiers in the Civil and Korean Wars didn't even shoot their rifles during battle. It was postulated that, even with human beings' capacity for violence, there is also something—compassion, empathy, responsibility, *something*—that was powerful enough to convince a significant number of men not to kill each other, even when the other side was trying to kill them. However, as we know, it doesn't take too long for compassion (and what we will come to know in Chapter 6 as "Self") to transition to *"I've got to do whatever I have to do, in order for me and my buddies to stay alive"*. That is a major component of basic training—to plant that seed when preparing for war. And unfortunately, there are times when there is simply no other choice.

I have a special place in my heart for the people who have fought for our country, and always reserve spots for them in my practice. While I question the *necessity* of wars such as Vietnam, I have no illusions about the *necessity* of a military force. Lt. Col. Dave Grossman once gave me a compliment—actually, a clarification of sorts—that has been one of the biggest gifts of my career. During a conversation after one of his presentations, he said to me: "Thank you for being a warrior." I sheepishly told him I was not a warrior; I was a therapist who often worked with veterans. He then said, "Well then, thank you for being a healer of the warriors." I never forgot that. I am quite proud and honored I can contribute in some small way, even if it is in my little office in Providence, RI.

> **TO CONSIDER:** What are your guiding belief structures and universal truths? Where did they come from? Do you/we ever make exceptions? (If we are human, the answer is yes.)

PART II

MY PATHS TO UNIVERSAL TRUTHS

It is my firm conviction that the path to fully embrace and embody universal truths is, really, whatever path works for you. In this next section, I will share some of the unlikely paths that led me towards the destination of responsibility, accountability, and civility.

CHAPTER 3

"IT'S FOR USE"—
THE TAI CHI STORY

I had some significant back problems for many years after playing drums, and my good friend and physical therapist, Greg Perkins, told me he had been taking lessons in a type of martial arts called Tai Chi. It had been extremely helpful for him both personally and professionally.

I had already had some experience with martial arts. When I was about was eighteen years old, I studied an American version of Karate, which involved the idea that one wanted to remain as hard as possible to shield oneself from the blows from others. Quite frankly, it was like the movie *Fight Club* on steroids. It was full contact, no holds barred, and either you hurt someone, or you got hurt. Oftentimes it was both. I stayed with it for quite some time, even though it was never a good fit for me. I did not like hurting my practice partner, and I certainly did not like being hurt myself.

Many years later, thanks to Greg, I finally found a martial fighting art that was not only a great fit for me, but an unlikely path towards so many of the things I was looking for in life.

The study of Tai Chi Chuan and the practice of being a psychotherapist have much in common. One of the main principles of Tai Chi, unlike in many of the other fighting arts, is to connect/touch with our practice partner or opponent, and to be able to maintain that connection for substantial amounts of time. This ability to connect with another human being is essential to being a Tai Chi practitioner, a therapist, or even just having a heartfelt conversation with someone. The practical use of Tai Chi paradoxically embodies compassion in that, being a self-defense focused martial art, the goal is not to win and make the other person lose, but rather to defend yourself and do only what is necessary to protect yourself and your loved ones from being harmed (essentially a Win-Win model, discussed later in this book).

To do this, great time and effort are spent in becoming sensitive to what is happening inside of us before we can truly be sensitive to another. Once we have spent considerable effort on exploring what is going on *internally* for ourselves, especially under stress, we can then begin an *external* exploration of what is going on inside our practice partner or opponent. That's when we can really hone our ability to respond and be able to connect, stick, adhere, and follow our partner or opponent wherever they may go. For more than twenty years, I have been drawn to Tai Chi's study of relaxation and power, integration of health and fitness, and the acknowledgement that the connection between the brain, body, and mind are inseparable. As my teacher writes: "Power and self-defense in Tai Chi are rooted in the organs, the fascia, the tendons, and the mind. Tai Chi is also the cultivation of health and vitality by enabling the body to become more supple and flexible, skin and muscles become better toned, weight normalized, and breathing becomes quieter, steadier, and more efficient. The curriculum includes softening exercises, barehanded forms, weapons forms, paired fighting forms, push hands training, restorative exercises and chi gung." (Training Tai Chi, Steve Brooks).

Shortly after my initial conversation with Greg, I started taking lessons at the Rhode Island School of Tai Chi. Master Teacher would often admonish us for being too tight and trying to "muscle" our way to overcome an opponent or practice partner. I would often hear him say,

"David! Why do you insist on using muscle! Why are you so tight! Why don't you make the decision to follow the PRINCIPLES?" He then would repeat the beloved and profound comment, "Why do you insist on struggling!" said softly, but with force.

I continued attending public classes, then private lessons, and eventually became an in-house student. After about two years, my back problems were alleviated, but I was struggling in a way that was reminiscent, yet contrasted, with the issues I had in my drumming years.

In my practice of Tai Chi Chuan, I had made a decision to start from the most basic levels of training and establish as firm a foundation as I could. One day I was working out with my practice partner Rick, and we were practicing a Two Person Form. It is choreographed, but acts as a basic framework for fighting, and incorporates the many principles of the Yang Family Style (the most practiced of the five family styles of Tai Chi) and teachings. At one point, my move was to punch Rick in his stomach/kidney (not a full strike), and Rick would catch my fist just before I struck him. He would then swing my arm down and to the side with significant force, and then strike me in the neck (this is called Slant Flying).

Usually, every time Rick would catch my fist, I would immediately tighten my arm, resist his next move, and make myself vulnerable for other strikes because I was so intent on preventing Rick from moving any part of me, or was trying to interrupt what he was planning to do. On this day I somehow said to myself, *I am just going to let my arm go, just try David, loosen, just let it go wherever it goes...* and it did! Rick caught my fist just before I punched his kidney, then he swung my arm down to prepare to strike me. My arm, using his momentum, followed the natural arc, came around, and my fist struck him in the chin. He had no chance to prevent my strike because all of the momentum and energy for *my* strike came from him. In physics we would call that potential energy converted to kinetic energy.

Rick said something like, "David! What the f**k was that!"

I responded, "Rick, I'm so sorry. I didn't mean to hurt you. I just let myself go."

I then realized something different had happened. I broke out of my usual routine of stiffness, muscle strength, and resistance. The light bulb went off: it was a "Hmmmmm, what just happened?" kind of moment. I asked Rick if we could try that again. I won't repeat exactly what Rick said, but the gist of his answer was, "Absolutely not!"

After the class I approached my teacher to recount this story. He said, "So you had a glimpse." I asked him to please explain. He said that people arrive here not knowing what Tai Chi Chuan really encompasses. So prospective students come to class based on faith thinking there may be something useful for them. Maybe their doctor told them they should move more; maybe someone saw something on television or perhaps in a movie that intrigued them about the practice. Most don't know the basic tenet that Tai Chi Chuan is based on Yin and Yang, soft and strong. The principles handed down by the Yang family take years of dedicated practice before one may even have a glimpse—the *Ah-ha!* moment. These glimpses are often fleeting, but if you have a way to *store* them, and you keep practicing, eventually you will begin to have more and more glimpses. That day he explained that the glimpses, which can accumulate over time, eventually become so substantial, that what was originally based on faith, leads to conviction. Twenty-four years later, I am a student of Master Teacher Conroy's first disciple, Steven Brooks, a true Master Martial Artist in his own right, and my conviction is truly embodied. However, I often still hear I am much too stiff and use too much muscle!

What I hope to convey with this experience is that the process of learning, whether it is the Yang Style of Tai Chi Chaun, or just about anything else, is universal. Those who embrace Tai Chi Chaun embrace responsibility by learning the fighting arts while having compassion for others, a strong sense of Internal Accountability for dedication to practicing daily for years, and External Accountability in trusting their teachers to evaluate them so they can grow.

It is not an easy process, much like being responsible (in general) is not often easy. In fact, to be responsible can be very challenging, especially when we are surrounded by so many counterexamples—from social media, from what used to be called "news", from entertainers to politicians, and from our current president, Donald Trump, who often name-calls, demeans, insults, and fabricates. President Trump is not alone in exhibiting this behavior, but I hope he too can have a glimpse and embrace some of the ideas concerning responsibility and lead the way for civility. In the way I had a glimpse during the two person set with Rick, we need glimpses of another way to behave and interact, rather than what is presented on much of television, media, or even by our president.

When we are looking for a glimpse, it makes sense to utilize the wisdom that has come before us. Plainly speaking, there is not much advantage in reinventing the wheel. The book, *Practical Use and Application of Tai Chi Chuan* by Yeung (Yang) Sau Chung is well known in the Tai Chi Chuan world, as it was written by Mr. Yang himself and provides glimpses into "the efforts of four generations." The translation from Chinese to English was also an arduous and challenging process, because words and symbols in Chinese don't necessarily translate to other languages. Great care was taken for the translation, and one of Mr. Yang's three daughters, Mary (Ma-Lee), gave meticulous consideration to the selections of words, phrases, and content. So, as students of the Yang style, we have learned to pay great attention to the language in this book. I am constantly amazed after twenty-four years of study how I, when I am lucky, experience something viscerally in my daily practice which was clearly articulated in the book, but I was not yet ready to embody it. The book establishes a foundation and framework to move forward. However, the book alone does not fully encompass this martial art. The quest of learning Tai Chi Chuan, and all its permutations, requires the oral and physical transmission of this information as well. Then, and only then, can your practice transform from theoretical to experiential. So the next chapter will explore the importance of real-life experience.

> **TO CONSIDER:** Think about a time you began something based upon faith. What was that experience like? Have you ever pursued something based solely on faith and it hasn't worked out? What has been your experience when you undertook something based on faith, which led to a glimpse, and then those glimpses eventually led to conviction? Does conviction seem to be connected to confidence? Can you jot down a few notes on this topic? Or how about writing just the "title" of it on a post-it?!

Theoretical:
The written word.

Experiential: The use of the written
word combined with the oral and
physical transmission.

CHAPTER 4

PRACTICAL USE AND APPLICATIONS OF TAI CHI CHUAN

There are numerous cliches about *talking* versus *doing*, such as: You can talk the talk but can you walk the walk; talk is cheap; actions speak louder than words; don't believe what a person says, believe what they do; etc. In Yeung Sau Chung's book, he emphasises that "incorrect postures are corrected and demonstrated on the spot." In fact, I have personally been told, "David, stop talking, and start doing." While Mr. Yeung's book is incredibly valuable, to become a true Tai Chi practitioner it is necessary to be taught (usually by a Master Teacher) the oral and physical transmission of this martial art. Once we have been granted the written, oral, and physical transmission, we as Tai Chi students have learned that then, and only then, can we not only talk about Tai Chi, but *more impor-*

tantly, apply it in real-life situations. Paralleling Mr. Yeung's framework, our goal is to be able to talk about responsibility, accountability, and civility—and *more importantly,* apply them in everyday life.

This concept is illustrated by a story often told in our Tai Chi school.

Many years ago, a Master Teacher, who was quite old, was teaching a class of students when a young man strode into the school and announced himself as a martial artist. This young man was not a student of the Master Teacher, nor did he belong to any affiliated school. The Master Teacher said nothing as the young martial artist went to the middle of the room and started to stretch his legs. Then, this young man started to kick the heavy bag suspended from the ceiling. This bag was *very* heavy, and it took a great deal of force to even move it a little bit. The young martial artist continued to kick the heavy bag, harder and harder, until the bag was moving in a way no student had ever previously observed. Then the young martial artist was spinning through the air (kind of like in the movie, *Crouching Tiger, Hidden Dragon*) in a way that seemingly defied gravity and resulted in even more ferocious kicks. It even *sounded* intimidating, like he was hitting the bag with a large wooden bat, WHACKKKKKK!!!!!!!! CRACKKKKKK!!!! Finally, the young martial artist shouted, "YOU!!!!! OLD MAN!!!! TEACHER!!! I CHALLENGE YOU RIGHT NOW!"

(In those days a challenge could lead to being maimed, death, taking over your school, etc.)

The Master Teacher said, "There is no need; everyone can see how powerful you are. You are indeed a worthy adversary." The young martial artist would not relent, and finally the Master Teacher got up from his chair and walked towards the young man. As they faced each other in the middle of the room, the Master Teacher appeared completely relaxed while the young martial artist looked like a wild tiger getting ready to attack. Then, with a primal scream, the young martial artist leaped through the air with a vicious kick directed right at the Master Teacher's face. Just before the young martial artist's foot connected, the Master Teacher moved his head barely two inches—just enough for the young martial artist's foot to sail past his face, and the young man's momentum continued to propel him forward through the air, as if he were gliding by on an invisible table and past the Master Teacher. Just as the young martial artist was almost at the end of his flight, the Master Teacher raised his hand to make contact with the forehead of the young martial artist and "gently" brought his head to the floor. The Master Teacher was very compassionate, because it can be a death strike if a person hits the back of their head on a hard unyielding surface. Although the Master Teacher was "gentle", the young martial artist was rendered unconscious on the floor.

All the students gathered round, stunned! They said, "Teacher, Teacher! How did you do that? He was so strong, he was so ferocious, he was flying through the air, he kicked the heavy bag in a way we have *never* experienced! Never have we seen such ferocity!"

The Master Teacher walked back to his chair quietly and sat down, not even breathing heavily, and did not initially respond to the students' questions. One student kept asking, "What just happened, what just happened, Master Teacher? Please tell us! How did you do that?"

The Master Teacher finally responded: "Well, he was very good at kicking the bag."

The moral of this story, and another universal truth is, *talking* about something is not the same as being able to *do* it.

> **TO CONSIDER:** When did you experience a transformation from talking about something (even if you have a great deal of knowledge about the subject) to being able to *do it?* How did that experience shape your life?

CHAPTER 5

THE DRUM MASTERS

"That cat can really play the skins!"
—*Just about any really cool jazz person talking about someone playing the drums in the '50's and '60's*

Louie Bellson

Louie Bellson

During my drumming years, there was (and still is) a famous music store in Boston, named E.U. Wurlitzer Music and Sound. They would sponsor clinics in which highly skilled and/or famous musicians would come to play and discuss their approach to their instrument. Louie Bellson was known as a musician's musician and was highly respected for his formidable drumming skills, keen musicianship, and his numerous recordings—including his work with the Duke Ellington Band. His work with this band, particularly, deserves a special note. At that time, segregation was in full force in our country. Even though Black Americans led the creation and movement of jazz, bands were racially segregated. Even if the bands and musicians were among the most famous in the world, even if their names were Duke Ellington, Count Basie, Louis Amstrong, etc., if they were people of color they would have to enter through a back door, could not use the bathrooms reserved for whites, could not eat at the restaurants, and could not stay at the hotel where they were featured entertainers. Using a white drummer in an all-black band was unheard of at the time. However, Mr. Bellson was a gentleman of the highest order. He wanted to play with the most talented people; he did not care what color or shade one was. In fact, he and Pearl Bailey (a Black woman) were married, and while I'm sure they ran into great obstacles, they were kind and gracious people and lived their lives together. Mr. Bellson was awarded just about every accolade a person and musician could garner, yet he remained humble—both as a performer and teacher. He traveled the country and taught young aspiring percussionists and veteran drummers alike. He came from a time when people, especially musicians, would say things like, "He's a cool cat." "Play those skins, man!", "That cat can really blow" (the trumpet), "Time to stir the soup" (play with brushes), and "I really dig that." (I still use that last one!)

One day in the late 1970s, I drove up to Boston to see Mr. Bellson at Wurlitzer's. The place was packed, and his famous double bass drum set was on two sheets of inauspicious plywood. He came out and started to talk about the bands and drummers that were part of the historical evolution of drumming and their influence in music—including significant figures like Chick Webb, Sonny Payne and Gene Krupa. He then brought out his snare drum and played a solo. What he could do on a single snare drum caused our mouths to gape open in astonishment. He then went on to his drum set and played several pieces that totally blew our minds. By the time he finished we were standing up, cheering, and clapping. He then talked about how he loves music and how he is "jazzed" by some of the younger drummers. He said he had heard a song on the radio, *50 Ways to Leave Your Lover*, by Paul Simon. All the drummers were talking about its unique drum part, which was rudimentary-based and performed by Steve Gadd. Mr. Bellson went behind his kit and played that two-measure phrase.

But this was the THING! Mr. Bellson said while his version was close, it did not have the exact feel that Steve Gadd exuded. Mr. Bellson also had an incredible curiosity—what Buddists call a beginner's mind: a mind that embraces a life-long quest for learning. Mr. Bellson had won the most prestigious awards possible, but his curiosity propelled him to reach out to Steve Gadd. Mr. Bellson found a way through his agent to contact this drummer, and he called him on the phone. He talked about how much he "dug" Steve's drumming and asked if Steve could tell him how he articulated that drum pattern. In my mind, the story is that Steve Gadd is blown away that Louie Bellson, **THE** Louie Bellson, is calling him and asking about a drum part! Steve Gadd suggested that they meet; Mr. Bellson agreed, and Steve Gadd showed Louie Bellson how to articulate that drum pattern. This young guy was showing one of the most famous musicians on the planet how to play his drum part. At the clinic, Mr. Bellson sat behind his kit and demonstrated how he originally played it and then how Steve Gadd had shown him. The difference was subtle, but made the groove and pattern flow in a unique way that caught your ear. (This way of playing has become a signature of Mr. Gadd's.) Now, I know I am belaboring the point, but, imagine, Mr. Bellson had done everything, won everything, and still had this thirst for more knowledge. I knew at that moment *I wanted to be just like that*, a life-long learner with an unabashed passion to explore. This was another seed. Later I spent a considerable amount of time reading about Mr. Bellson and how he, by example, advocated for Blacks. Throughout his life he demonstrated a sense of responsibility to give credit to Black drummers and musicians for the creation of jazz, when others did not. He was one of the most civil human beings I had ever met and embodied the universal truth that all people are *deserving* of being treated with dignity and respect. Nor did he talk about it, or sermonize us, he just lived it! He was one *cool* cat!

Steve Smith

During the late '70s and early '80s, our band was touring more and more, and playing concerts with our original material. One song we recorded began to get some airplay on the radio, and we played up and down the east coast. We were what musicians used to call "road warriors." When I first joined the band, we played about twenty-eight nights in a row! Our regular schedule was to perform at least five nights a week, often six, and that did not count travel. During the summer after we recorded our album, Bobby (The Guid) Decurtis (the band's lead tenor sax player) and I traveled to California to promote the album. We stayed with Scott Jackson, a former drummer of our band. The Guid had arranged a meeting with a distant relative, Bruce Conti, who wrote the *Rocky* theme song, and had/has a prolific composing, arranging, and conducting career. In addition, he often conducted the orchestra for the Academy Awards. We met Mr. Conti, who was very gracious, but it did not lead to our band getting picked up by a major music label.

Steve Smith

Sometime after we returned from California we had a break in our schedule, and I thought it was time for another drum clinic. Steve Smith was the drummer for the band Journey—for a time, one of the most famous bands in the world. He was conducting a clinic at Wurlitzer's Music Store in Boston. While Journey was ultra famous, Steve Smith was not known at that time as a *drummer's drummer*. I wasn't really thrilled about going, but decided at the last minute to make the trip. Mr. Smith began the clinic by talking about how important it had been for him to explore the history of drumming, and to study those who came before. (Many years later, he would publish a teaching CD named *Standing on the Shoulders of Giants.*) He talked about the influence Max Roach had on his approach to the drums. Mr. Roach was a jazz drummer extraordinaire: his solos could be constructed like a song with an intro, verse, chorus, bridge, and back to the verse, etc. His technical skills, feel, as well as his creativity, were also extraordinary. Many of us had listened to Mr. Roach, but I would guess most of us couldn't play those types of solos—I certainly could not.

During the clinic, Mr. Smith said he would like to pay homage to Mr. Roach by playing one of his solo pieces. He then sat down behind his drums and played a beautiful rendition of a Max Roach solo. While this was not a lights flashing, fire-coming-out-of-the-stage type of solo, we were stunned by the eloquence of the arrangement. The next piece he played was one he wrote as an homage to Max Roach, yet with more of a rock concert feel and volume. Mr. Smith then played a piece called "KEROPE", which incorporated all kinds of influences, rebound techniques with his drumsticks, Mr. Roach's song structure, time feels, and double bass figures. By the time he finished with a flurry of bass drum kicks and cymbal crashes, we all went crazy with spontaneous cheers and a standing ovation. Mr. Smith was very humble and gave several thank you's. Then he said, "I just want you to know I'm not depending on my best day to play this piece."

I quickly thought, "What a conceited person! Now he's going to tell us how good he is." Was I wrong! He went on to talk about how we all are a product of those who came before us, and how practice, study and *discipline* are all essential elements of developing a level of *competence* that does not require your best day to do whatever it is you want to do. He then discussed many of the people he had studied with (including Gary Chaffee!) and the many techniques he utilized. Again, drums brought another life lesson to me: Discipline. Looking back at my time as a drummer, I had demonstrated a form of discipline by practicing so many hours on drums, but I lacked the personal responsibility, and therefore—an honest appraisal of what I needed to improve on. In addition, I was unable (or unwilling) to utilize whatever tools or people that could help me move towards my goal. Another seed!

Not surprisingly, Steve Smith is known worldwide today as a drummer's drummer, Master Teacher/Clinician, and a great player who apparently never stops learning, embodies discipline, and is still humble.

Buddy Rich

I met Buddy Rich when I was about twelve years old. Buddy Rich was one of the most famous drummers in the world, and was able to do things on the drums that no one has been able to do before or since. While his drum solos amazed even the most proficient percussionists, he also had an ability to swing and drive a band with a signature sound and time feel.

Amazingly, Buddy Rich was famous for letting people know he did not practice; nor did he believe in practicing. He believed you could either play or not. Mr. Rich did acknowledge he listened to others, and they had an influence on his playing. He was also a regular on several of the talk shows in the 1970's that dominated late night, and he was often referred to as "The World's Greatest Drummer." Mr. Rich also brought a bit of sarcasm and wit to these shows that the hosts and the television audiences enjoyed. I had been hounding my father for years to play drums to no avail, but my Dad finally said, "If you want to play drums so badly, I'll take you to see the best."

Buddy Rich

My father got tickets for us to see The Buddy Rich Big Band, and we went to Nottingham Village for the show. Somehow my father maneuvered us into a back hallway where suddenly, I saw Buddy Rich passing by right next to me. I reached out my hand and said, "Hello Mr. Rich," and Mr. Rich shook it briefly. I still remember how small his hand was and the feel of the soft muscles between his thumb and forefinger. I then asked, "Could I ever have a pair of your drumsticks after your performance?" Mr. Rich launched into a tirade, "What? What did you ask for? Why would you ask me that! Those are my tools! Would you ask a carpenter to give you his tools out of his toolbox? Would you want his hammer?!" I was speechless, and my father was too. I remember Mr. Rich's last words as he walked away, "This is why I don't come to these shows early!!"

As upset as I was I was still amazed at his and the band's performance. But I learned another life lesson. I promised myself that if I ever did get to play drums, I would try to be kind to people if they wanted to talk to me. I knew **_I didn't want to be like that._** Another seed. Later, it became well known that Mr. Rich could be verbally abusive, and a member of

The Drum Masters

his band even made recordings of Mr. Rich yelling, screaming, swearing, and physically threatening the members of his band while on a bus.

Before the internet, these recordings were not widely distributed, but many musicians knew about Mr. Rich's temperament. Later, when the tapes became widely available, they became infamous, and parts were even used in an episode of *Seinfeld*—the number one comedy at the time. It was played for laughs on TV, but if you listen to those original recordings of Mr. Rich berating, threatening to harm, swearing and insulting members of his band on the tour bus, there is nothing funny about them.

The behavior of Mr. Rich also presents a very intriguing aspect of responsibility and accountability. While Mr. Rich could clearly be very abusive, there are also many stories of him having deep friendships, being a loving husband and father, and having significant appreciation for people in the jazz world. Mr. Rich's polarization of two distinctly different ways of treating people more accurately reflects the capacity of how we, as human beings, can behave. This may not feel great to acknowledge, but it's true.

> **TO CONSIDER:** What kind of impact do you have, overall, on those around you?

PART III

THE PSYCHOLOGICAL UNDERPINNINGS

CHAPTER 6

OVERVIEW OF THE INTERNAL FAMILY SYSTEM MODEL

I am respectfully offering the Internal Family Systems Model as a potential path to a more collective embracing and embodiment of responsibility, accountability, and civility. I do not believe, in any way, it is the *only* path. There are many paths to pursue these universal truths and principles, and if you've found that a different path or road gets you there, great! Hopefully, we can unite in that our *destination* be the same. I, and many others, have found internal family systems to be unique in its construction and unlike many other psychological models, very accessible in its language and concepts.

The Internal Family Systems (IFS) model, developed by Dick Schwartz, Ph.D. with the collaboration of his many clients, and significant contributions by colleagues, is a non-judgmental model of psychotherapy: a template for living our life in a connected and compassionate manner, and a paradigm of mind. IFS embraces the concept of the "multiplicity of the mind" in that at our core exists the entity of "Self" (with a capital "S") and we are also composed of many "parts." A helpful analogy for those not familiar with IFS would be that of a professional sports team. The Self is like the head coach on the team and the "parts" are like the players. The head coach is the leader of the team but at times, the parts can also have the autonomy to make their own decisions on the field. Ideally, if the head coach trusts his team, and the team trusts the head coach to lead them, they all will have a much more harmonious relationship, take responsibility for their respective roles on the team, and treat each other with civility and respect. In addition, great teams that endure over time are anchored with a foundation, framework, technology, and the required tools to be successful. We have all witnessed what happens when coaches, players, and management are not on the same page. I believe IFS provides a solid foundation and framework for our internal system to work together, and as doctors Dubin and Schwartz state in their interviews in this book, IFS provides the *technology and tools* to address and heal our inner system. When we have a harmonious internal system, parts can return to their *natural valuable state* (being a team player) and trust that Self (the coach) is capable and invested in providing calm, confident, and compassionate leadership as needed.

Self and Parts

The Self has many names: the Buddist Mind, the soul, our core, essence, Holy Spirit, etc., and refers to something that is on board when we are born. Dr. Schwartz and Dr. Sweezy describe the Self as having "all the necessary qualities of good leadership, including compassion, perspective, curiosity, acceptance, and confidence. It does not have to develop through stages. As a result, the Self makes the best inner leader and will engender balance and harmony inside if the parts allow it to lead." (Internal Family Systems Therapy, Richard C. Schwartz and Martha Sweezy, second edition, 2020 p. 38).

Parts, in the language of IFS, are described as a family of inner people that reside in us. For example, I might have a younger part that can throw caution to the wind, and an older part that realizes I don't heal as well as I used to after bungee jumping. Both parts feel *very* different. Doctors Schwartz and Sweezy write: "Parts behave like internal people of different ages, temperaments, and talents and respond best when related to as such." p.282

The Self is further described as embodying the 8 C's. The 8 C's are reference points to help determine when we are more fully "in *Self*," or alternatively, when we are more fully "in a part." Being more fully in Self or being more fully in a part are separate states, but are interconnected.

When we are in Self, it is an identifiable state, a certain kind of *feeling*, during which we embody those 8 C's. It is an aspect of being a human being. In the martial arts we call that Chi or *gi;* Dr. Schwartz commented to me once in conversation that Chi is Self-energy. When you're playing in a band there is a very similar experience, a *feeling*, when everyone locks into the same wavelength and something synergistic happens. The individual musicians meld into a unit, becoming more than the sum of our individual parts. We call this phenomenon "being in the pocket", "in the groove", or "locked in". It always felt to me like the separate instruments and musicians became one big locomotive.

There was the experience of being closely connected to my bandmates and intimately connected to the audience as well. This experience of being linked to something bigger than yourself is an important aspect of IFS and Self. It's not an intellectual exercise, and you don't have to be a musician or study IFS to *feel* it either. Just think of a great concert you attended, and that one point when you, the audience, and the band became one thing, *connected.* (For me, that would be seeing James Brown at Brown University; Earth, Wind, and Fire at the Providence Civic Center; Stevie Ray Vaugh and Double Trouble at Providence Performing Arts; Huey Lewis and the News at the Providence Civic Center; and playing in the same show as James Cotton, and getting a lesson from his drummer (Mr. Kenny Johnson) on how to play a *real* shuffle.) Or watching a game in a sports bar or crowded stadium, as *your* home team wins a championship! Or what it feels like to volunteer and be part of a united effort to help victims of a natural disaster such as a hurricane, flood, or wildfire.

A critical mass of Self means we more fully embody the qualities such as compassion, perspective, and being centered than we would if we were "in a part." Dr. Schwartz appears to be drawn to alliterations, and while many have suggested other C words, or words that begin with other letters, the 8 C's have continued to provide a beautiful template for differentiating when we are being led by Self (the head coach) as compared to being led by the parts (the team).

The 8 C's are: **CURIOSITY, CONNECTION, COMPASSION, CLARITY, CALM, COURAGE, CONFIDENCE,** and **CREATIVITY.**

As I mentioned in Chapter 1, it's surprising how often a gap exists between one person's understanding and another's of a word or characteristic, so I would like to highlight three of the C's in particular: Curiosity, Compassion, and Courage. (For a more comprehensive exploration of these qualities, refer to the book *Internal Family Systems Therapy* by Richard C. Schwartz and Martha Sweezy, and/or the *IFS Skills Training Manual* by Frank Anderson, MD; Martha Sweezy, Ph.D.; and Richard C. Schwartz, Ph.D.)

Curiosity: All of us have experienced curiosity about something. But how about when that *something* is at odds with our thoughts or belief systems? Do we tend to be more curious about it, or less? Michael Elkin (my IFS teacher and mentor) has taught me more than anyone when my curiosity is diminished, it's a good bet I am usually in a part, and my part may not give a flying hoot about the consequences of my behavior or listening to someone else. I have found, when I am not curious, that is usually the end of a productive conversation. Michael Elkin has a very practical description of the *process* of being curious. He states that having curiosity "means you don't assume you know the meaning of something until you have made an inquiry, and then we attach meaning to it."

Compassion: For me, compassion includes the concept of interconnectivity within yourself and between others, and it often folds in well with the word kindness—involving a desire to do something *for*. It can feel quite similar to empathy—the difference being, with empathy, that I am identifying *with someone or something*, and though it can be incredibly heartfelt, I'm not necessarily going to do something about it or *for* them.

IFS differentiates compassion from empathy on a neurological level as well, referencing research by neuroscientist Tania Singer, which concludes that these two seemingly similar emotions involve different neuropathways in our brain. Dr. Singer defines compassion as *feeling for* another person, and empathy as *feeling with* another human being. However, just like the Tai Chi symbol, these two experiences are not totally independent.

In addition, IFS distinguishes the difference between compassion and pity. These are very different. Pity can include a level of what can *seem* like compassion and empathy for someone or something, but also interwoven in the experience is a level of distaste, repulsion, and/or disgust.

Courage: From ancient legend to modern-day entertainment, our heroes are usually portrayed as having courage. Courage is often viewed as having little or no concern for your own personal danger or risk. Casually walking away from a blown up building in slow motion, utilizing some unique method or weapon for inflicting pain or death, or delivering a quippy catch phrase as you vanquish the villain makes it seem as if courage happens in the absence of fear, trepidation, consternation, dread, vulnerability, panic, regret, etc. I believe it is usually the opposite—that courageous acts often happen *in the presence* of those very things—and yet the person does it anyway. Or, as we learn in trauma and Polyvagal Theory, maybe a person can't respond, and that doesn't make them any less courageous. (For more on this, see the books by Dr. Stephen Porges and Deb Dana, LCSW on Polyvagal Theory, and Lt. Col. Dave Grossman's exploration on *The Psychological Cost of Learning to Kill in War and Society*, listed in the biography.)

Parts

Parts also can be conceptualized as subpersonalities—individual beings who have their own history, experiences, perceptions, age, gender, values, roles, jobs, etc. For instance, the feeling and energy of my musician part are very different than my martial art/protective father part. Parts have their own ways of interacting with our own internal system, and also with *Self*.

Parts are divided into three main categories:

Managers: The parts of us that look to keep the homeostasis/balance of our system by managing the other two categories (Exiles and Firefighters). The Managers often believe that if those parts we call Exiles (which carry experiences of hurt, embarrassment, trauma and shame for the rest of the system), were to be fully heard, they would overwhelm the system. So Managers spend an enormous amount of energy trying to prevent that, doing their best to keep the Exiles out of awareness, submerged, or completely banished. In addition, just like in any profession, Managers can be kind, supportive, mean, abusive, helpful, critical, stressed, or only be concerned with results, etc. When our leadership role, (who is in charge), is fulfilled by the three part system in these types of situations, The Managers have an impossible task to keep the Exiles out of our of awareness, and/or keeping the Firefighters from charging in to quell the inevitable Exiles' emergence with little or no regard for the ensuing carnage. When the shit hits the fan (and it will), the system will lose its tenuous balance point. Eventually, without Self in the leadership role, the three-part system will do its best to regroup (hopefully), and the Managers will return to their job and mantra of "Never again." Yet, despite their honorable intentions and their Herculean efforts, they eventually tire, and the cycle continues.

Exiles: The parts of us that carry the burdens of trauma, shame, worthlessness, etc. They often contain our earlier/childhood experiences. Bessel Van Der Kollk, in his landmark book *The Body Keeps the Score* (2014), articulates the many ways in which we encode trauma physiologically, psychologically, and neurologically. We find that painful memories and experiences from the past, affect our present and future experiences, despite the efforts of the Managers and Firefighters who are given the task of keeping the Exiles at bay and/or out of our awareness. The Exiles have a thankless task because for true healing to take place, they *must* be heard, and as Ann Sinko, LMFT (see interview in Appendix B) states: "fully seen and understood" before they can be healed and transformed.

Firefighters: The parts of us that emerge and "come to the rescue" when all else fails and the Exiles have escaped, or maybe there is merely a wisp of their presence that is detectable. The IFS term "Firefirefighter" does *not* reference this heroic profession the way that we are used to. Both types of firefighters have an honorable intent. However, in IFS, these Firefighters completely take over and send the Exiles back to where they came from—with extreme prejudice, you might say. They too have a thankless job. When I talk about the effects of Firefighters, I use the example of Civil Rights Protesters being blasted by fire hoses and sent flying into walls, smashed to the ground, and often severely injured. When the Firefighters are pressed into action, they will do anything possible to send the Exiles back to a place where they cannot disrupt the internal system. There is often a disregard for the ensuing carnage because the Firefighters feel the Managers have failed to keep the Exiles at bay, and they (the Firefighters) had to fight for the life and death of the internal system.

Burdens

Burdens are the negative beliefs, experiences, cognitions, and body memories an Exile, Manager, or Firefighter takes on (or absorbs) often from childhood and/or trauma. These beliefs often include, "I'm worthless, I'm defective, It's hopeless, I'm helpless, I'm shameful, I'm bad," etc. In addition, the parts that absorb these experiences are frequently "frozen in time" and we/they re-experience these states in cognitive, visceral, behavioral, neurological, physiological, and relational experiences in present day life. (Note: For those who want to delve deeper into this subject matter, see the Bibliography for several books which I have found helpful.)

No discussion of Burdens would be complete without mentioning Michi Rose, Ph.D.: LMSW. Michi Rose has been, and continues to be, a seminal figure in IFS's origin and continued development. Among her many contributions was her incorporation of the process of *unburdening*, an absolutely essential aspect, into the IFS model.

While the Managers and Firefighters can carry burdens, it is often the Exiles that are convinced these beliefs and experiences are the *definition of who and what they are*, rather than *something that has happened to them*. It's an enormous difference. If you *are* your Shame, your Trauma, your past transgressions, etc., it usually is experienced as immutable.

Protectors

One of the roles Managers and Firefighters undertake, or are given, in an effort to keep us functioning in everyday life and in some form of balance, is to *protect* us from experiencing intense feelings such as shame and trauma. Exiles are most often the main repositories of shame and trauma. Protectors, both Managers and Firefighters, experience Exiles as a threat and will have a host of strategies to keep them subjugated, and out of awareness. Yet, Exiles, despite the efforts of the Managers and Firefighters, continue to rise up and through to be heard. It is almost as if they realize the need to be fully seen, understood, and unburdened as essential for the internal system to return to a Self-led balance.

Protectors often have a thankless job as well. Lastly, there is some debate in the IFS community about whether a protector, or protector energy, can be Self-led. I believe it can if the part has a critical mass of Self-energy. For example, people such as Dr. Martin Luther King, Susan B. Anthony, and Nelson Mandela fought many battles for equal rights and fair treatment. They all had a mission to *protect* the people they represented. I believe they were *very* angry about the injustices they, and the people they represented, had to endure. These visionaries took their protective energy and anger and channelled it to a positive, unifying, and transformative force.

GOALS OF IFS

1) To help parts release their burdens so they can find their preferred roles in the system.
2) To reestablish trust in Self-leadership. When Self is in the lead, it respects input from the other parts, who in turn respect Self to effectively lead the system.
3) To achieve balance and harmony within the internal system.
4) To affect the external system to have more Self-energy.

(The Center for Self Leadership (2006) Level 1 Program Assistant Manual)

Overview of the Internal Family Systems Model

However, when the three-part system, as opposed to Self, is in the *primary* leadership role—as honorable as the parts are and despite their efforts—the internal system will be caught in a cycle of ongoing pressure that will lead to difficulties. It goes something like this:

- The Managers are often working around the clock to keep the system running; they are often exhausted.
- The Managers will utilize many strategies to contain the Exiles, but eventually the Managers will falter, and/or the Exiles will somehow emerge or escape.
- Like any oppressed group, Exiles are frantic to tell their story in many ways, including non-verbally through body sensations (as explored in *The Body Keeps the Score*).
- At this juncture, the Managers may have to double down to remove the Exiles from our awareness and/or the Firefighters may take over.

The end product of the 3 part system in the leadership role is illustrated in the following situation:

- The Managers are upset with the Exiles for emerging in some way and angry at the Firefighters for overreacting.
- The Firefighters are angry with the Exiles for disrupting the system and are frustrated with the Managers for not doing their job.
- The Exiles continue to be oppressed by both, subjugated and isolated with incredibly heavy burdens to bear that *need to be healed*.
- At this juncture, the three-part system *paradoxically* regains its homeostasis/balance until the next time.

And the next time will come! Because the irony is that until the Exiles are healed, or what we call *unburdened* in the language of IFS, they will continually rise to be heard in some way. If this process sounds familiar, it may be because this is the same dynamic of racism and oppression.

For me, one of the life-changing concepts of IFS is that *all* our *parts* have a positive intent for the internal system. They are trying their best to keep the status quo, keep us safe, and keep us in a state of homeostasis, or balance—even if that balance is off kilter. Why? Because they believe the alternative is so much worse!

Let me provide an example that could be helpful. I do a lot of work with people struggling with substance use. A woman—let's call her Sarah—came to see me because she was drinking two bottles of wine per night, has been on an administrative leave from work due to being intoxicated, has two Driving Under the Influence arrests, and has experienced significant difficulties with her partner. In our first session I began by taking a thorough history. Not just because it is an aspect of good practice, but because I am always looking for what might be the "core fuel," as I refer to it. The core fuel in this situation would be *why* a person may be drinking at a harmful level. Many believe that harmful substance consumption is often a *symptom* of something rather than the actual core fuel. There are exceptions of course. Sometimes it's as straightforward as a person "just" developing an incremental dependency on a substance, but in my experience that is fairly rare. Sarah's alcohol use, seen through the lens of IFS, would potentially point towards a Firefighter, who as we have described, protects this person from something perceived as far worse than all the troubles continued alcohol use has contributed to in her life. What could be worse? What could be worse than drinking is the escape of an Exile(s) carrying shame, trauma, pain, humiliation, defectiveness, etc.

"Shame" is capitalized because it is a powerful force in our internal system. Like radioactive material, it can have a half life of thousands of years if not addressed. Michael Elkin, LMFT describes Shame as "our badness witnessed by others."

For a much more comprehensive review of Shame, please look up Dr. Brene Brown's famous Ted Talk, "The Power of Vulnerability" and her videos and books. She calls Shame "the most powerful, master emotion. It's the fear that we're not good enough." It "corrodes the very part of us that believes we are capable of change."

So, for Sarah, if Shame could be a factor, what 'benefits' could this level of alcohol-induced anesthetization deliver? Usually, with this level of alcohol consumption, a Firefighter is using any means possible to keep the Exile, and what it carries, out of our awareness. This Firefighter does not care about the negative effects of their behavior—they are only concerned with numbing our bodies and minds so we don't have to feel the intolerable feelings, memories, or experiences the Exile(s) carry, *especially* Shame. Alcohol can send the Managers off-line or on a break. In addition, very little effort (lifting a glass) can provide seemingly instant relief to the intolerable pressure the three-part system experiences when it is in the leadership role under these circumstances. Unfortunately, there is a very high price to pay for such a short-lived reprieve.

The substance use cycle goes something like this:

- There is an Exile, or Exiles, that carries the burdens of the past, usually Shame-based, and serves as the core fuel.
- The Firefighter, in an effort to dull the pain, will use a substance that has these analgesic properties for relief and will also diminish the pain or numb the Exile out of awareness.
- This strategy—and it *is* a strategy—leads to behavior which usually generates even more Shame, such as driving under the influence, court appearances, troubled relationships, etc.
- When the 3 part system resets, the Manager's mantra of "Never again" becomes the driving force of the internal system. Never again: *will I drink, will I over-drink, will I drink before 3 pm, will I wake up drunk, will I drink and drive, will I drink and drive with the kids in the car, etc.*

However, with the three-part system in the leadership role, it is almost always an impossible task, and the Manager becomes like Sisyphus in Greek mythology—cursed for all eternity to push a huge boulder up a mountain side only to have it roll back down again just before he got to the top. Sarah and I looked for the core fuel and succeeded in discovering that what was called *discipline* during her childhood was actually emotional and physical abuse. Sarah was and is very courageous to journey down that path to truly heal the parts of her that were profoundly shamed and had endured so much.

On a lighter note, this is another story I tell my clients to help explain this idea of *parts*.

When our daughters were younger, my wife and I would take our three girls to the beach, and we used to play a game called "Acid Seawater." (Seeing it in writing now makes me think I might have given the game a different name.) I would be in the ocean with Samantha, Emily, and Christina, and they would splash water towards my face, and I would yell, ARHHGGGGGGGGGG, ACID SEAWATERRRR!!!! I can't SEEEEEEEEEEEEEEE! Then, while pretending to be unable to see, I would try to find them while they circled around, usually JUST missing catching them while they laughed and continued to splash me.

At this point in the story I would tell a client I was in a *part*. That part was like an eleven-year-old playing, laughing, making believe he couldn't see and being fully in the moment.

But then, a wave comes and slams Samantha, and she is pulled underwater. I go from being about eleven years old, to an adult who used to be a lifeguard and is now calculating how far she traveled with the force of the wave, evaluating the angle of the surf, getting a visual on Christina and Emily to make sure they are safe, wading to a spot I think Sammy will be be carried to, remembering the color of her bathing suit, seeing it, reaching down and grabbing Sammy, and pulling her out of the water. I check to see if she's alright, and she is! I check for Emily and Christina; they're good! Ah, everyone is safe. Then Sammy points to the water and says, Daddy, what's that? I look down and Sammy splashes me in the face, I grab my eyes—Aiiiiiyeeeeeeeeee!!!!!! ACIDDDDDD SEAWATER!!!!!!!!!!!!! I am transported back to being 11 years old again, and all of us return to the game. What joy!

Now if an alien was analyzing us, they may say:

> "The life form that identifies as an adult human was playing with those little humans saying, 'Ayieeeeeee... Acid Seawater!!!!!,' and when splashed, that adult human grabbed his visual spheres like he was being harmed, but we can detect no damage to his optic center circuitry. According to our charts on human development,

this adult human acts like it is 11 or 12 years old. But, the human who was yelling, 'Acid Seawater' looked *exactly* like the human who retrieved the little female human after it was submerged underwater. *This* human was very serious, calculated the angle and trajectory of the wave, tracked the little human, and pulled her out of the water. They look the same, but they must be different. Our spectral analysis shows this adult human's brain waves, physiology, adrenalin levels, and computational skills were completely different."

What conclusion would these aliens come to? There must be *two* human life-forms who look exactly alike! Later, the aliens might learn they are mostly right, but instead of observing two different human life-forms playing with their girls, they really observed two distinct *parts* in one human life form.

> **TO CONSIDER:** When did you have a *feeling* of confidence and calm in a situation that was challenging? What was the feeling in your brain, your body, and your heart? What was it like when you were so blended with a part that it felt like that part was the totality of who you are? Could you jot down a few wonderful experiences of being blended, and also when being blended with a part was not so wonderful?

CHAPTER 7

COGNITIVE PHYSIO MECHANISMS

In this section, I have fused aspects of the Psychoanalytic model of defense mechanisms; the Cognitive Behavioral Therapy (CBT) model of cognitive distortions; and the inclusive models of researchers such as: Bessel van der Kolk, M.D.; Judith Herman, M.D.; and Francine Shapiro, Ph.D; regarding the importance, impact, and necessity of integrating physiology in the practice and study of psychology, especially trauma.

A defense mechanism is an internal mechanism to protect or shield ourselves from unwanted thoughts, feelings, and behaviors. A cognitive distortion is similar to a lens (or mechanism) through which we view, interpret, and experience the world in a negative way.

I call the product of this fusion a Cognitive *Physio* Mechanism because our physiological systems (i.e. Neurological, Nervous, Muscular, Circulatory, Endocrine, Immune, Renal, Respiratory, and Skeletal systems) are all interconnected. They are all subsystems, or parts, of our whole system. Thus, our cognitions, though they may *not* result in observable behavior, do have a direct effect on our internal physiological systems and vice versa. I believe this mechanism can be another useful tool for understanding why universal truths and compassion can so readily be undermined or completely circumvented. Conversely, understanding these mechanisms can help us to be more compassionate to ourselves and others, and to regain our footing when we have gotten off track or lost our way.

All human beings process information in both our mind and body, and this amazing synergistic apparatus is made up of separate but interrelated components, which combine to form one integrated system. A car is another example of this type of process, and in some ways, human beings are very similar to cars. Both are self-contained, composed of many mechanisms that result in one complete functional system, dependent on a specific amount of air and fuel, and at their best when there is regular maintenance and repairs. In addition, for optimal performance, the driver, mechanisms, and system will work together in an integrated and harmonious relationship.

A mechanism is designed to have things work in a manner which has a very predictable outcome. When a Cognitive Physio Mechanism is engaged, regardless of what goes in, the erosion of responsibility, accountability and civility are the likely outcome, and are experienced in both our minds *and* our bodies.

Parts utilizes this process, as compared to *Self*, which does not. Remember in the previous section on IFS, parts have a positive intent and can embody a great deal of protector energy in our internal system, especially when they are in the primary leadership role. Thus, Cognitive Physio Mechanisms are paradoxically very valuable to protector parts in our internal system because by definition, they shield and protect us from the reality and effects of our thoughts, feelings, behaviors, and consequences—especially when we violate the rights of others.

If that makes sense to you, then the identification of a Cognitive Physio Mechanism, just like Dr. Schwartz's 8 C's, can help us become *curious* about what *parts* are involved, and what purpose that mechanism has served in our past or present experiences.

I have defined three Cognitive Physio Mechanisms (CPMs), which are particularly important when we diminish or abdicate the universal truths such as responsibility, accountability, and civility. They are: justification, rationalization, and blame. (Appendix A includes more on the structure of CPMs and the definitions of 3 additional mechanisms: denial, minimization, and dichotomy.)

Justification is a CPM whereby a person shields or protects themselves from unwanted thoughts, feelings, behaviors, and consequences by invoking a higher good (often God). Justification is an especially dangerous CPM because its use often circumvents compassion, curiosity, discussion, or logic. Think of all the harm done by people who quote their religious texts to support oppression, subjugation, and murder. Justification is also an instrument that is utilized in almost all wars, because when we are preparing for war, the model is to objectify the "enemy" and to instill that we are fighting against them for our country, freedom, or liberty—all high, noble goals.

This is not to say all wars are unnecessary. There are people and regimes that violate every tenet of human dignity, responsibility, compassion, and accountability: the Khmer Rouge and Pol Pot, Fidel Castro, Kim Jong un, Idi Amin, the genocide of the Indigenous Peoples of North America, the horrors committed to Black people in our country, Hitler and the Nazi party, and the list goes on.

Justification is a formidable excuse and mechanism for name-calling, ethnic slurs, objectification, and marginalization. Not surprisingly, this mechanism is embraced by all coercive regimes. Once a person, culture, or group is reduced to a derogatory name, a slur, or a thing, it is relatively straightforward to justify their subsequent subjugation and oppression. For a very powerful example of the impact of words, you may want to watch Spike Lee's movie, *Do the Right Thing*. There is a scene when the actors (in character) look straight into the camera, and say all the ethnic slurs and insults available at the time, with the visceral and emotional charge that accompanies these derogatory words. You will *feel* the power of words after watching *Do the Right Thing*.

Rationalization is a CPM whereby a person shields or protects themselves from unwanted thoughts, feelings, behaviors, and consequences by constructing an explanation which could be plausible, but is actually inaccurate. So in other words, it could seem to make sense, but in the full light of day would not measure up.

Here's a personal example which might help. When I was a student at the Community College of Rhode Island (CCRI), I was asked to be part of the student organization that was in charge of providing entertainment for the students. We had a surprisingly large budget and could hire up-and-coming national acts. We did a significant amount of work, researching, contacting, scheduling, and hiring bands to play. One day, another person and I were lamenting how much work we were doing WITHOUT being reimbursed for our time and efforts, sometimes fifteen or more hours a week, for months at a time. For several weeks we talked about how it wasn't fair at all, and we became more and more resentful. We began to think and feel it was absolutely within our rights and fair to have some type of compensation for numerous months of work, especially when other staff at CCRI were certainly being paid for their jobs. Eventually, we decided we *would* be paid for our significant efforts. I and another person took about $400 each. This is an example of rationalization. I was stealing. I stole. Even now, 35 years later, I get a sick feeling in my stomach writing this. When I accepted this position there was never any suggestion I would be paid for my time. It was 100 percent volunteer. And I 100 percent stole that money.

Some weeks after stealing the money, I got called in to meet with Dr. Ron Schertz, the Dean of Students. He asked if I knew anything about some discrepancies in the accounting of the Student Entertainment Organization. Even at this early stage of my attendance at CCRI, I had come to respect Dr. Schertz, so I hesitated for a moment, and then told him I had taken the money. I don't think I could bring myself to say the word "stole" during that conversation. I offered to make full restitution (and did), and realized I had lost my sense of responsibility and Internal Accountability. I felt ashamed of myself, and knew I abused the trust that was invested in me by Dr. Schertz and others.

I also experienced something different with Dr. Schertz. Instead of bringing legal charges or expelling me from college (all of which would be understandable), he continued to guide me. He never sought to shame me, and we developed a friendship over time. In IFS language, we would say Dr. Schertz was in Self.

Blame is a CPM whereby a person shields or protects themselves from unwanted thoughts, feelings, behaviors, or consequences by abdicating their/our own responsibility, and holding another person, culture, color, thing, etc. responsible. Instead of looking inward, it is a consistent view outward. Blame is not a labor-intensive mechanism, because its function absolves us of any causality. Blame usually results in the death of curiosity. As Dr. Dubin stated in her interview in Appendix B, "it's very, very satisfying, temporarily, to blame." Interestingly, IFS has a technique called taking a "U-Turn," which is, instead of looking out and blaming someone or something else, you circle back and explore what's going on inside of *you*.

CHAPTER 8

INTERVIEW WITH RICHARD SCHWARTZ, PhD

I respectfully offer IFS as a potential path to responsibility, accountability, and civility. Again, IFS is not the only path to attain these universal truths. But I believe IFS is unique in its construction and its accessible language of parts, its application to real life, and its ready-made foundation, framework, technology, and tools required for our quest. For those not conversant in IFS, or who have embraced an entirely different path, I include here an interview with Dr. Richard Schwartz, the founder of the Internal Family Systems model. Further interviews with Ann Sinko, LMFT; Rina Dubin, Ed.D.; and Michael Elkin, LMFT can be found in Appendix B. Even if IFS is not your path, I wholeheartedly encourage you to read their interviews as well. While the template for my questions for the interviewees were the same, there are very special observations made by all such as: Ann Sinko's reflections on white supremacy and her expertise on the impact of legacy burdens; Dr. Dubin's observations regarding the importance of context, and deference to authority; and Michael Elkin's unique lens, moral meaning, and his answer regarding the question, "Do you believe that a standard of responsibility and civility has eroded in our country?"

I connected with Dr. Schwartz when he consented to work with an individual I was seeing in my clinical practice who was diagnosed with Schizophrenia. I had introduced IFS to this young man, and his treatment was starting to gain some traction in a way it never had before. However, I was only in my first year of IFS training and not fully confident in my skill set, and knew that seeking advice from a more experienced IFS clinician would be a huge asset. So I sought out and joined a consultation group led by Ken Jaeger, LICSW, CGP (who is highly skilled in IFS), and it was he who suggested I may want to ask Dr. Schwartz if he would be willing to work with this young man. I attended an IFS Trauma and Neuroscience training in Chicago that Dr. Schwartz, Dr. Frank Aderson, and Fran Booth, LICSW were conducting. During a break in the training, I shared with Dr. Schwartz a brief history of this young man and how IFS had been so helpful in our sessions. Then I pitched my request and asked if Dr. Schwartz would join me in working with this person. He said, "Yes, I'll do it. Let's talk when we return," in his very reserved manner. I, *not* being very reserved, said, "Thank you, Dick," waited until he left the table, and once he was out of sight, jumped up, and did a dance and several fist pumps.

I had the honor and privilege to collaborate with Dr. Schwartz and this young man for over a year. Dr. Schwartz was willing to teach me, and eventually became a mentor as well. The transformation of that young man over the course of that year was nothing short of amazing, and I believe IFS represents a paradigm shift in how we can address seemingly intractable mental health concerns. I believe we, as behavioral health providers, have a personal responsibility, and are accountable to the people we work with, to not always look for an answer via psychopharmacology/medication. As for that young man, well, he's doing great! And he, for me, embodies the word courage.

Interview with Dr. Dick Schwartz

DAVID: I'd like to talk about some of the ideas about being responsible and accountable and what that might be like from a personal lens, and also through the lens of IFS. And are they the same? From your personal perspective, how would you define responsibility?

DICK: Well, this has been a big problem in our culture because the idea of personal responsibility goes back to the idea of self-control and will power, and all that is part of what I call the *burden of individualism* and that we should be able to control ourselves. If we can't, it is our fault and is a personal weakness and failing. Therefore, we are not taking responsibility for our actions. So, in our work, so many people feel a bias (judgement) with that attitude and tear into themselves because they couldn't stop drinking; they couldn't stop smoking; they couldn't stop yelling at their spouse. And then they have this critic that is chiming in with the party line of: *you're worthless, you're shit because you can't control yourself, and you should take responsibility for yourself.* And that would just make them feel more worthless, and the Firefighter would have to do even more to get them away from the shame.

And at the same time, when people have access to their Self, they can have, "will power" in the sense that when parts want to do something that isn't healthy, Self can just say, in a gentle way, *You know, I don't think that's the best idea; we're not going to do that today.* But, it can be hard to do until they [a person's internal system] can get to that point. Then, at that point, they would be responsible. Responsibility is the ability to respond. But until they got there, it's just fodder for the critics saying, *You should have personal responsibility.*

DAVID: Even that word [Responsibility] is kind of like a slippery slope. At least one of its definitions is the ability to know between right and wrong, and to be accountable. I think the slippery slope is when judgment [from the critic] seeps into the system. It's a very different interaction when the three-part system is in a leadership role, as compared to what you later described: a decision stemming from a critical mass of Self.

DICK: Yes. I mean generally, that [definition of responsibility] just fuels the critic who already is black and white and moralistic, and the more the critic gets going, the more burdens and shame you carry, which requires extreme Firefighting. So, that is the dilemma we are stuck in when we try to control impulses.

For instance: [a person may say to themselves], "*Yes, I have a part that did that, and I'm going to work with them so they don't keep doing that."* But it isn't from a, *"I'm a total worthless shit for doing that"* lens.

DAVID: One of the topics I look at is internal and External Accountability. And in IFS, experiences and behaviors are something that can be influenced externally, but it's our internal system that is the reference point.

DICK: Yes. The goal is to achieve Self-leadership which really means good inner parenting, that you are able to discipline your parts in a loving way, to remind them of what's healthy for the system at times, carry a vision that [all parts buy] into, and how you want to live your life. Negotiate so parts have a voice. It all ties into good Self-leadership, which then leads to the ability to be responsible.

DAVID: Do you feel that a standard of responsibility and civility has eroded over time in our country, and potentially our world?

DICK: Yes. It's all parallel. What is happening in our country parallels our leadership and how most of the leaders are very polarized themselves. So, anytime a system becomes highly polarized, then civility goes out the window. Because protectors, especially Firefighters, don't care about collateral damage; they don't care about who they hurt that much. They just do their job. Then, the protector parts of other people react to them, and it just becomes protector wars, no Self to be found, and yes, that's the end of civility.

DAVID: The definition that I use for civility, at its most basic level, is merely refraining from rudeness and being polite in a perfunctory way. Then there are different levels of civility. But when civility has eroded, and there are decisions made by people, families, and leaders that they are *not* going to be civil, it's a very different kind of interaction.

DICK: Yes, and the definition you gave is a very managerial kind of civility, but it is better than the free-for-all right now.

Interview with Richard Schwartz, Ph.D.

DAVID: What would be your, or an IFS definition, of civility?

DICK: Ideally, it would be a Self-led kind of civility where you are civil to someone because you respect them and you know there is Self in them, and you know whatever extremes are driving them come from pain—from their Exiles. So you treat them with respect and compassion, even when you are standing up to them. Even when you are stopping them from doing what they are doing. That is Self-leadership.

DAVID: And how would you suggest someone would interact with [the president] and if you don't want to be quoted specifically about President Trump, let me know,

DICK: I do not have a problem with that.

DAVID: Ok. So what are your thoughts when a person, or his parts, have really abdicated the description of civility you described, or even at the most basic level that I described. And that person is so blended with those parts. What are your thoughts at that juncture?

DICK: Even with someone like Trump, when I can stay in Self, I can see past his crazy protectors, the little boys inside him that are driving all of that feeling totally worthless, empty, and desperate. So I can have compassion for him, but at the same time, I am going to do what I can to stop him and get him out of office. So he's a good example of what we're talking about; you don't have to build up a lot of hate for someone to motivate you to actually stop them. You can stop them from [a position of] Self.

DAVID: That seems to dovetail with examples such as Dr. Martin Luther King, Susan B. Anthony, Nelson Mandela, and how they have been the instruments of enormous change. However they didn't use hate as the motivation. In fact, it was reconciliation despite the level of oppression they, and the people who they were representing, had experienced.

DICK: Yes, they are good examples of what we are talking about.

DAVID: Do you have any other examples of people that you look to that have those kinds qualities?

DICK: Ghandi is not the best example because he was nasty to the people around him, even though he advocated for non-violent protests.

DAVID: I must admit, If I were in jail for 27 years, wrongly accused, like Nelson Mandela it would be a tough sell that I would promote reconciliation.

DICK: Yes. Someone was just telling me a quote from Eldridge Cleaver. He spent a lot of time in solitary confinement and he said he wouldn't wish it on anybody, but it was the best thing that ever happened to him because he really had to find himself... and in our language, really work with his parts.

DAVID: Do you believe in the innate good in people, and if so, how do you grapple with the fact human beings, usually men, in all countries and cultures continue to oppress and subjugate?

DICK: Yes, [this happens in] the absence of IFS. There is this inherent Self; it's all good, and that is actually in each of our parts. But trauma forces parts into extreme roles and burdens them and leaves them stuck in the past, and so they become quite extreme from where they started from, which is their natural valuable states. And they carry these impulses that burden them and can drive them to do heinous things, but it is not who they are. It's not their essence. And those burdens can be unloaded, and when they are, they transform back into their natural valuable states. So, for many, what may be thought of as evil comes from trauma and is in the burdens we carry after that. That is not at all human nature or parts nature.

DAVID: And why such a discrepancy between men and women?

DICK: I think several reasons. 1) Men in general, because of patriarchy, they have a lot more power to oppress. 2) Men have this little extra squirt/bit of testosterone that not only makes them hornier, but also much more aggressive. When you combine that with certain kinds of burdens, then that makes men much more aggressive. 3) Men are brought up in a culture, male culture, where to survive you have to be aggressive often. So they look to those Firefighters when they get triggered. 4) The fourth is that men, much more than women, are socialized to exile many more parts. The more parts you exile the more extreme your protectors have to be.

DAVID: Lastly, Hope is an essential aspect of the IFS model and the human experience. In IFS we frequently refer to being a "Hope Merchant" in the therapeutic process. What do you hope for: for yourself, for your country, for the world?

DICK: I hope that at all those levels, we use this pandemic to reorganize the individual level of our system of parts, that we are able to step away from the parts of us that have been driving us to these extremes, that we change the way we treat the earth and each other, that we can learn that we don't need nearly what really thought we needed, that we can enjoy the downtime we have now, and that we can be a lot more respectful to the earth and to each other. I do think this is some of what this pandemic is about. The earth is giving us a chance to wake up and recalibrate so we can continue to exist, because the next wakeup call might be a lot more... bad.

DAVID: Michael Elkin has an expression about the irony of the universe. Do you remember it?

DICK: What he says is, *Irony is the driving force of the universe.*

DAVID: Yes, yes, the driving force. It's ironic that instead of nuclear bombs, biological warfare, the thing that brought the entire world to halt is this tiny little microbe, and has reset everything.

DICK: Yes, there is some irony in that, but if you go to the big picture of it, it is what is called a homeostatic mechanism, in the sense that you see the earth as a living system and we all have homeostatic mechanisms to keep our blood pressure at certain levels, our body temperature, our glucose levels and so on. So when we get out outside of some range of those things, there are feedback loops that kick in that brings us back, and with the planet; our level of population growth; our unrestrained growth, both economically and in terms of incursion; of deforesting; things like that, has released. This is just the first series of viruses that are coming because of our intrusion into wildlifes' habitat—these are homeostatic mechanisms designed to scale us back, so we don't continue to be such a cancer to the planet. So, my hope for the planet is that we get the message, and that we change so we treat it better.

DAVID: What do you hope for our country?

DICK: That we get the message, and we wake up, and we move away from the goal of unlimited growth and base our ideas of success on that measure, and learn to live with a lot less.

DAVID: And would you say civility, as you described it, would be a necessary component?

DICK: The larger picture is, those goals I mentioned earlier are hard, very hard to achieve unless people heal. So it all ties back to healing these traumas that drive these extremes. And civility just happens naturally once that happens. As you unburden, it releases Self, and your Self is inherently civil.

DAVID: I guess what scares me is, we have leaders that don't embrace that—even at the most base level that I described—and that has really energized those parts in other people.

DICK: That is contagious. Protectors are contagious. But, Self is also contagious. So the more Self we can bring to this planet, the more everything will calm down even though it doesn't look good at this moment. So, even if you are doing it in your office, with your Self, it does add to a force-field of Self, and it can have that effect.

PART IV

THE REAL WORLD

CHAPTER 9

OPPORTUNITIES LOST

Let's look at 3 examples of real-life, high-profile situations involving some very well-known, and quite powerful, people. These individuals carry enormous influence when it comes to the overall tone and tenor of society. We will delve into how quickly people such as these can abdicate responsibility and accountability, and even more concerning—miss an opportunity to learn a valuable lesson.

Michael Pence, Vice President of the United States of America

In July of 2017, our Vice President, Mike Pence, visited NASA. At one point he was able to personally view one of the Orion prototypes that had travelled to the moon. Prominently displayed on the capsule was a sign that stated, "Critical Space Flight Hardware," and just below that, "DO NOT TOUCH." In a now infamous photo, Vice President Pence is shown with his hand clearly on the Orion space capsule. The most telling aspect of this incident is not the Vice President's transgression (which was minor, especially in comparison to his boss's actions), but his casual deflection after the media uproar. The Vice President sent a message out via social media that stated: "Sorry @NASA...@MarcoRubio dared me to do it!" Sheesh. He may as well have added an "LOL."

A NASA representative then tweeted, "It was okay to touch the surface. Those are just day-to-day reminder signs. We were going to clean it anyway. It was an honor to host you." I believe NASA issued a "soft" response in an effort to not have their funding reduced.

The NASA incident resolved itself and was "handled" in a more or less glib tone by the VP, and what I imagine to be a forced casualness by NASA. And while this didn't result in damage to equipment, a critical malfunction, or the injury or death of an astronaut, think about the message that was sent by the breaking of that simple rule, and by Pence's reaction to having been called out on it. After the photo was published, it would have been so easy for the Vice President to tweet: *Regarding that photo when I visited NASA, I made an irresponsible choice. That sign was there for a good reason and I set a very poor example. I should have been more conscientious, and I apologize to NASA.*

When I observe an incident like this, I really work at not judging a person for making a mistake, but I pay close attention to what our elected leaders do, especially after having made a mistake, regarding responsibility, accountability and civility. Sometimes what they *don't* do is just as telling.

I'm referring here to Vice President Michael Pence's position, or lack of a definitive one, on what is called conversion therapy. Conversion therapy is predicated on the belief that loving someone (romantically) who is the same gender is wrong. The Bible is often quoted as the unassailable reason (i.e. justification) to discriminate and persecute same-gender couples. A same gender relationship is purported to be an affront to God. In this interpretation of the Bible, and conversion therapy, being gay is a "choice." Implicit in the word "choice" is that being gay is the *wrong* choice.

So let's extrapolate using Socratic Logic with a major/minor premise and conclusion. Because being gay is a choice, and being gay is the *wrong* choice, conversion therapy will "help" a person, often a child, reorient to what is *right and what God has intended*. Conversion therapy's goal is to reorient a person back to their *correct* relationship with God and sexual orientation, i.e. heterosexuality. Given conversion therapy's premise that having a same-gender attraction is wrong, actually a sin and an affront to God Himself (God is evidently male), its methods are harsh, corersive, and shaming. The American Psychiatric Association (APA) on November, 15, 2018 stated: *The APA opposes any psychiatric treatment, such as* "reparative" or "conversion" therapy, that is based on the assumption that homosexuality per se is a mental disorder or is based on a prior assumption that the patient should change his or her sexual orientation.

For Clinical Social Workers, The National Committee on LGBT Issues asserts that conversion therapy or any form of attempting to change the sexual orientation and gender identity/expression are an infringement of the guiding principles inherent to social workers' ethics and values, a position affirmed by the NASW policy statement on "Lesbian, Gay, and Bisexual Issues" (NASW 2014). In 2014 the American Medical Association's Journal of Ethics addressed the unethical practice of conversion therapy. In 2020, the American Medical Association (AMA) updated their previously established position: "The AMA has advocated to ban the practice of so-called "conversion therapy", a harmful practice which attempts to change an individual's sexual orientation, sexual behavior or gender identity. The practice of pathologizing and "changing" sexual orientation or gender identity is not supported by scientific evidence. To the contrary, evidence has shown that "'conversion therapy' is harmful, contributing to increased suicidal behaviors and psychological distress" (AMA Advocacy Update. June, 2020). Despite these condemnations, conversion therapy was still allowed and practiced in Vice President Pence's home state of Indiana, where he served as a member of congress from 2001 to 2013 and as governor from 2013 to 2017. In 2019, a bill was submitted to ban conversion therapy for minors by Representative Chris Chyung and Senator Mark Stoops. It did not pass.

Lastly, it may seem a sharp left turn to mention Tai Chi at this time. But I want to highlight something I believe is important, and directly related to our current Vice President. There are 13 essential rules to this martial art. Number 11 is, "Action is included in inactivity." In the context of Tai Chi, this is a positive. Unfortunately, Vice President Pence embodies this axiom all too well. I contacted Representative Chyung in late 2020 and asked if conversion therapy is still permitted in Indiana. Not only did he confirm it is still permitted, but it is *still* permitted to be used on children as well. Imagine, this "therapy", which is not a therapy at all, is still permitted despite the fact that it dehumanizes, oppresses, and negates the humanity of our most vulnerable population: our children.

DAVID MEDEIROS

Former President William Jefferson Clinton

Universal truths like responsibility and accountability are at the heart of human values. They remind us of the difference between right and wrong, and the idea that we are answerable. The following examples, of a former president and a talk show host, offer poignant comparisons of the Principle of Responsibility with one crucial difference.

In 1999, at the time of former President Bill Clinton's impeachment proceedings and video testimony, I was facilitating court-mandated Domestic Violence Groups for men—most of whom had been physically violent, as well as verbally, psychologically, emotionally, and financially abusive. Let me tell you, the responsibility concept was a tough sell for these men to buy into. Conversely, blaming the victim was something almost all of the men tried in an effort to abdicate responsibility and accountability for their actions. In addition, there is a strong correlation between escalating levels of blame and escalation of harm and violence. I have worked with over seven-hundred men in these groups and I have never, and I mean never, heard about someone who hurt their partner while telling them about all their good qualities and what a wonderful person they are.

Part of the structure of our agency was a weekly "check in," during which each group member would describe what they had done to their wives, girlfriends, or partners. Initially, the facilitators/I would work with these men to define what abuse is and develop a list of abusive behaviors. Eventually, we would have a very substantial list and then have a vote on whether they would be willing to use the list to identify their own behaviors. This stage of group development was quite intense, and we would spend a lot of time on developing a consensus. Once we did, we would vote and establish a verbal contract which would provide a framework for talking about *what abuse is* and then move to constructing a foundation upon which the responsibility concept could be built.

As we developed this list we would invariably talk about relationships. The men often defend an affair as *not* abusive. Janis A. Spring, Ph.D., in her book, *After the Affair*, defines an affair as a "breach of trust." I often use her definition because it is not unfamiliar for people to debate what constitutes an affair in an attempt to minimize its effects and risks to their partner.

In early January of 1998, Clinton was deposed regarding allegations made by Paula Jones that she suffered psychological damage as a result of him exposing himself to her in an Arkansas hotel room in May of 1991. (TIME)

During this process information was leaked about a possible relationship between President Clinton and White House intern Monica Lewinsky, and Ms. Lewinsky was subpoenaed and subsequently deposed by Paula Jones' attorney's, in an effort to demonstrate a pattern of harassment in the workplace. On January 25, 1998 Clinton ended a televised speech by stating: *"But I want to say one thing to the American people, I want you to listen to me. I'm going to say this again, I did not have sexual relations with that woman, Ms. Lewinsky. I never told anybody to lie. Not a single time. Never. These allegations are false, and I need to go back to work for the American people. Thank you."*

As Clinton walked away from the podium he received a round of applause.

During 1998 Clinton was called to testify twice. On August 17, 1998 he testified before a grand jury and made the infamous statement, "It depends on what the meaning of 'is' is." That sentence has been googled millions of times as a sound bite, but the sentence alone lacks the context of the entire response: "It depends on what the meaning of 'is' is. If the— if he—if 'is' means is and never has been, that is not-that is is one thing. If it means there is none, that was a completely true statement. Now if someone had asked me on that day, are you having any kind of sexual relations with Ms. Lewinsky, that is, asked me a question in the present tense, I would have said no. And it would have been completely true."

Following his grand jury testimony Clinton televised a speech to the nation acknowledging that, "indeed I did have a relationship with Ms. Lewinsky, that was not appropriate, in fact it was wrong." Just days later the Supreme Court rejected Mr. Clinton's claim that as President he should have immunity from civil cases. This ruling enabled the Paula Jones harassment case to proceed against him. (*The Guardian*, Bill Clinton Clinton Impeachment Timeline, Nov 1998). President Clinton was impeached by the House of Representatives in 1998, in the context of having previously lied under oath/committed perjury, and consistently abdicated his personal responsibility for the affair.

I have included this lengthy story and timeline because I believe our leaders, especially our president, whether we believe it or not, have an enormous impact on our moral compass, and a duty to demonstrate a sense of responsibility, accountability, and civility. I feel confident it was not a 'civil' conversation after Ms. Clinton had stood before all the nation and the world, defiantly defending her husband. I will never forget the many discussions for over a year and a half with the men in the Domestic Violence Groups referencing Clinton as a role model, and attempting to disparage Hillary Clinton. After President Clinton's use of semantics, obfuscations, and the infamous "meaning of *is*" video testimony, I personally witnessed an even more substantial change in the domestic violence/abuse group's attitude and direction. Their mantra was now, "If the president of the United States can do it, what's the big deal?" Such an opportunity lost!

Let's compare that to the *Late Night* talk show host David Letterman. He too, was outed for having had an affair/relationship, but with a fundamental difference. On October 1, 2009, Mr. Letterman began his "apology" by acknowledging, during his televised show, that he had sex with staff members. It was a very awkward disclosure and I believe the audience did not really know if this was a new skit or joke. Letterman spent considerable time telling the audience that a person had tried to extort him and threatened to leak the information if he did not pay a huge sum of money. Letterman expounded about enduring the hardships of going to law enforcement and subsequently testifying before a grand jury. I am not sure if he was truly trying to apologize—to share how he himself had been violated by the extortion attempt—or to get ahead of the story. He did apologize to staff members who may have been hounded by the media for more information.

On October 5, 2009, Mr. Letterman addressed his behavior for a second time, again during his televised program. He began by saying "I'm terribly sorry" to his staff who have been incredibly supportive through the years. Then there was the apology to his wife, Regina. "She has been horribly hurt by my behavior, and when something happens like that, if you hurt a person and it's your responsibility, you try to fix it. And at that point, there's only two things that can happen: either you're going to make some progress and get it fixed, or you're going to fall short and perhaps not get it fixed, so let me tell you folks, I've got my work cut out for me."

There it is: responsibility and accountability all in a concise statement. If Mr. Letterman could have stayed with that content, it would be a robust example of the type of apology we are talking about. However, these three sentences were embedded in the middle of his speech, and at the end Mr. Letterman veered off course. Rather than judge him for it, I choose to see this as an example of how difficult it is to stay on course during the process of apologizing. I think we have all apologized to someone during which we found a reason to divert attention and protect ourselves as well. Those types of apologies do not usually resonate for the person we are apologizing to. To Mr. Letterman's credit, the second time he addressed his behavior he did include an apology that took responsibility, accountability, and a stated effort to "fix it."

Contrast Mr. Letterman's statements with some of former President Clinton's comments when asked if he had apologized to Monica Lewinsky. He responded, "I apologized to everybody in the world." The word *obfuscate* is often referred to when discussing the former president. I'm not sure what apologizing to every person in the world entails. Later, in an interview on the *TODAY Show* in 2018, Clinton was asked repeatedly, had he ever *directly* apologized to Ms. Lewinsky. He eventually acknowledged, "I have not talked to her. But I did say publicly on more than one occasion that I was sorry. That's very different. The apology was public." Yes Mr. Clinton, that was quite different.

So, in the Domestic Violence Groups, I used Clinton as an example as what could have happened if the President was in *our* weekly meetings, did some work, and was held accountable by the other members of the group. It could have gone something like this:

President Clinton decides to seize the opportunity, hops on board a time machine, goes back in time, and holds a televised press conference. Instead of, "I did not have sexual relations with that woman," he says: "My fellow Americans, I am appearing before you humbled and quite frankly, embarrassed. I am acknowledging an affair with a staff person publicly, for implicit in my office, and my personal life, is an expectation and duty to provide leadership and set an example at many levels. I was wrong and I take full responsibility for my actions: I've got my work cut out for me, and I am going to do that work. Thank you and good evening."

The result: a speech defined by responsibility and accountability. If President Clinton had been able to do this, I truly believe his personal legacy (becoming a model of responsibility and accountability) would have transcended, even eclipsed much of the collective good facilitated by his administration. Imagine googling that speech to regain your course.

When facilitating Domestic Violence Groups many years ago, I used to believe my proposed apology for President Clinton was based on a foundation of responsibility, accountability, and ethics. Looking back, I believe I was *wrong*. If we shifted the contextual framework a bit, former President Clinton's behaviors may have been interpreted quite differently then, and especially now. For instance, what if instead of being the President/CEO of the United States, William Jefferson Clinton was the CEO of one of the most influential and successful corporations in the world.

Let us extrapolate: the CEO of this international conglomerate is somehow involved in hiring a young woman, as an intern no less, just out of college, with little or no experience. Despite the CEO's incredibly busy schedule, and needing to consult with the top experts domestically and internationally, the intern would have unprecedented access and proximity to him. This CEO eventually had some type of sexual relationship with her. In addition, because this CEO is so well known, he would have to have a professional security force to ensure his safety. The security force would know the CEO is married, would be aware something is happening outside of the CEO's marriage, would have to lie directly or by omission to the CEO's wife and family, and would have developed a strategy to be worked out so the wife/partner of the CEO would not be allowed in the private office when the CEO might be otherwise engaged. There would also be some way of the CEO communicating an "all clear" message for staff and security personnel to return.

If we were to integrate President Clinton's behaviors into the CEO framework I have just proposed, it would look quite different. The most powerful person (man) in the world making advances towards a 21 year old intern. It could not have been a more unequal power differential. Ms.

Lewinsky has reflected on this very dynamic in articles she has written. Lastly, if I was doing a risk assessment for the corporation, I would postulate this CEO was displaying a selection and grooming process, knew how to stay just inside of the law, (and while still "legal" I wonder what the public perception would have been if the young intern was 19 years old), and postulate this was not the first time something similar had happened. Now some people may be saying to themselves, "This guy (me) *doesn't* think this type of behavior goes on everyday in the corporate world? How naive!" Actually, I *know* it goes on, and that's the point! *It continues to go on.* And it *wasn't* an "inappropriate relationship." It was an abuse of status and an abuse of power.

"Interestingly," in yet another interview as reported in Time Magazine, 4 (2018) former President Clinton, "when asked if he felt he owed [Lewinsky] an apology, said, 'No, I do not." The weirdest part of it all: an irreverent and irascible talk show host provided a better example to start the process of taking responsibility and being accountable. I wish it had been our President.

Me

Sometimes, in my professional life, clients share that they can't imagine me angry, and really losing my you-know-what (shit). I reassure them this is not the case, and if clinically indicated I may share this personal story as well.

Our daughter Emily was about 5 years old and we were going to run some errands. I was stressed for some reason and had asked Emily several times to get in the car. Emily continued to sit on the stairs that led to the garage. Well, I have had great parental moments with Emily, but this was not one of them. I raised my voice and started to say something like, "Emily, let's goooo, come onnn!!!" Then I started tethering between a raised voice and yelling. "What's the matter? Let's gooooo! Emily…what's the MATTER!?" I was becoming increasingly upset, angry, red faced, getting in her face and now definitely yelling, "Let'ssssss GOOOOOOOO! RIGHT NOW!!!! WHAT'S THE MATTER WITH YOU!!!!" And then, "WHAT THE F**K!!!!?"

Emily's eyes filled up with tears, and she remained frozen to the spot. Then I blamed her for not getting up while I was yelling at her. By this time Emily was sobbing. This, by the way, this is not fun to write at all. I don't remember if we ran the errands or not, what I do remember is that night Emily was terrified of me—and to be quite frank—for quite some time after. I knew somewhere deep down I really had messed up. I tried to talk to Emily that night but I was still in a blaming frame of mind (or part) and just failed miserably. I tried again the following day.

This is about how the conversation went:

ME: Emily, I want to talk about yesterday.

EMILY: I'm sorry Daddy, don't be mad at me. [Ohhh, I still feel that one.]

ME: Actually Emily, Daddy really messed up yesterday; it didn't matter what you did, or didn't do yesterday. Daddy was wrong to yell at you like that.

EMILY: I was scared, you scared me, Daddy. (Tears start to well up in her eyes.)

ME: I know Emily, and if you want to talk about it, I will.

EMILY: It was really scary, you were screaming at me, and when you got close I got really scared.

ME: Too scared to move... and I was still yelling at you?

EMILY: Not yelling... you were *screaming* at me!!! (Now tears are streaming down.)

ME: (A pause—"Yelling" sounded so much better than "screaming." Rationalization and Minimization to the rescue.)

ME: You're right Emily, Daddy was screaming at you; that was wrong.

[Resisting the urge to say, "If you just came when I asked I would not have to scream at you!" TOTAL BLAMING. And it was my Shame over my behavior that made me want to blame her. Thankfully, I refrained from saying that.]

ME: You're right Emily, Daddy was screaming, and there is no reason to treat you like that!

EMILY: I was really scared!!!!!! (More tears coming down her face.)

ME: Daddy doesn't want to do that kind of stuff, so I am going to talk to someone who has helped me with that before. This wasn't your fault, Emily.

EMILY: *She stopped talking. She did not want to talk anymore.*

I wanted it to be over but it was not. Emily continued to be terrified of me for quite some time, and it wasn't unusual for me to be in this flux and vacillate between frustration and Shame, back and forth, around and around my parts would go. It would loop like this: If I raised my voice, or was tense, I would see fear in her eyes, and I would usually feel Shame for what I did to her, then I would start to think about how long this was going to go on, then frustration/blame would ensue, which didn't feel *nearly* as painful as Shame, and I could stay in the Frustration Zone and on The Blame Train. Until, it started all over again—I had to do a lot of personal work to change that pattern.

I have come to understand that some of the core fuel of my anger and rage was from how I was raised. My mother and father loved me, and I have come to believe they really tried, but had their own unresolved trauma histories. The effects of being traumatized and shamed was not unfamiliar for them, and unfortunately not unfamiliar for me as well. I did not want to recreate those aspects of my childhood and was really aiming to be a great parent. I was not able to meet that mark. I came to embrace a much more realistic concept. For me, it is the wonderful concept of D. W. Winnicott, who coined the term "good enough mother."

My interpretation of "good enough" means that great is just not a realistic goal, and that it takes an incredible amount of work just to meet the standard of "good enough."

When I talk about this with clients, I sometimes share a condensed version. I let folks know we *all* have moments or times in our lives when we are far from being Self-led. And if these times were shown on a Jumbo Tron screen at a big sporting event, we *definitely* would not define ourselves as great. If appropriate, I may also share I usually *strive*, and often *struggle*, as a father, husband, and person for "good enough." These "opportunities" often feel like shit, but are incredibly important for ourselves, and those around us.

At the end of the day it is not fame, status, or laws that insulates us from Shame, embarrassment, or failure; it's looking into our own internal system feeling we have done the right thing and acted accordingly. And when we haven't done the "right'" thing, and that happens to **all** of us because we are all human, we can learn to lead from Self and apologize in the way Dr. Schwartz and I discussed in his interview: "It is important to repair things when your parts take over and do extreme things, and to apologize and take accountability. For instance: [a person may say to themselves] *Yes, I have a part that did that, and I'm going to work with them so they don't keep doing that.*"

> **TO CONSIDER:** How do our leaders take responsibility and accountability, or not, for their mistakes? Do they apologize in a way that resonates with you, or do they even apologize at all? Do you believe our elected leaders—such as the president and vice president—have some type of duty and responsibility as role models, given they are two of the most powerful and influential human beings on the planet?

Opportunities Lost

Names left to right: Steve "The Kid" DeCurtis; Bobby "The Guid" DeCurtis; David Carbonara; Bobby "Bobby Mac" Mancini; Tommy "TJ" Schwartz; me; Kevin Cason; Steve Smith in the foreground.
Photo courtesy of Bonehead Music Inc. dba Steve Smith and the Nakeds.

Me

On stage for the very first time.

Opportunities Lost

The first time I played a drum was in Pawtuxet Rangers Fife and Drum Corps.

Mr. Eddie Watson, my—and so many others'—beloved Voice Coach.

My family, left to right: Samantha, me, Christina, Tricia, and Emily. At the Women's World Cup soccer tournament; USA vs. Germany; Quebec, Canada

Everett: Company Stage & School. Left to right: Tiana Whittington; Joseph Henderson; (in rear) Aaron Jungels, Co-founder and Co-Artistic Director; me; Dick Schwartz; Grace Bevilacqua; Justine Jungels Bevilacqua; and Laisha Crum. on stage after their performance of Good Grief at the National IFS Conference in 2019 in Colorado. They received a standing ovation, and then asked Dick and me to join them.

PART V
—

CAUTIONARY TALES

"What I do know is that there is 'response'
in responsibility... responsibility is the key word."
—*Elie Wiesel,* Night *(p. xv)*

"Never in my life would I have ever thought we
would need a law to make this happen."
—*Henry Parish III, Mayor of Cocoa, FL*

CHAPTER 10

WHAT CAN ERODE A SENSE OF RESPONSIBILITY, ACCOUNTABILITY, AND CIVILITY?

On July, 9, 2017, a disabled man in Brevard County Florida was drowning in a retention pool as five teenagers looked on. They "mocked, laughed at, and recorded a video that was later posted online." In addition, "the teens can be heard laughing at Mr. Dunn, telling him he is going to die and they weren't going to help him as he struggled and screamed." In subsequent interviews in the media, people commented on whether these young men/teenagers did something illegal. Interestingly, these young men did not break the law—not only of Florida, but in most, if not all states. Jeffery Lapin, an attorney in Nebraska, commented about this incident, "While it is morally and ethically wrong, it is not illegal to not render aid or make extremely despicable comments."

What a stark example of the erosion of responsibility, accountability, and civility. Actually, this incident shows a complete abdication of those universal truths. It is easy to vilify these young teens, and I believe what they did was despicable. But I can't help but wonder: what's their moral code? Do they even have one? In our analysis, what these young men did, or did not do, was technically legal (meaning they did not violate the law) but also morally deplorable. These young men demonstrated what happens when personal responsibility, accountability, and civility have been diminished to the point of not being remotely visible at the precise moment a fellow human being was in mortal danger. The theoretical ramifications of the erosion of empathy and compassion became experiential for Mr. Dunn, and are compellingly evident. Mr. Dunn died in that retention pond.

Would a law obligating bystanders to help someone in danger have been effective? Possibly. Possibly not. I personally don't believe it would have. These universal truths and moral values are more powerful when they come from *inside*. That is what ethics are. I am not saying laws are unimportant, but we have laws prohibiting murder, and yet we have one of the highest levels of handgun and firearm related homicides in the world.

Bad Leadership/Role Models

The first presidential debate took place on September 29, 2020 between President Donald Trump and former Vice President Joe Biden. During this first (and only) debate, President Trump definitely demonstrated he does not embrace being civil, even at its most rudimentary definition. His postings on social media are laden with: name calling, insults, labeling, demeaning language (especially towards women), and taking credit for most of the progress while blaming others (often former President Obama) for the difficulties our nation faces. He has referred to Elizabeth Warren as "Pocahontas" after she stated she was Native American, when she is not. He coined nicknames for Joe Biden, former Vice President of the United States and presidential candidate, including "Lunch Bucket Joe" and "SleepycreepyJoe." He often calls people "crazy" and then adds their name. Trump was video taped in an interview where Senator John McCain, and a former POW in Vietnam, was part of the discussion. Trump comments about Senator McCain: "He's a war hero because he was captured. I like people that weren't captured. I hate to tell ya." I would like to believe this would be absolutely unacceptable to anyone who served our country, nor their families. It is absolutely unacceptable to me.

What Can Erode a Sense of Responsibility, Accountability, and Civility?

Our president may think being civil is for wimps, that he knows what's involved in being imprisoned and tortured in a POW camp, and that name calling and lobbing insults is a sign of confidence and power. It can be powerful, but I challenge you to find an example of when it has been powerful in a positive and transformative way.

The people who we choose to represent us have significant power and influence. The famous experiments on obedience to authority conducted by social psychologist Stanley Milgram in the 1960s demonstrate how an authority figure—and I will extrapolate, *our leaders/our president*—can influence and shift a person's moral foundation in a very short period of time. This is a cautionary tale indeed.

After the clash between White Nationalists (really White Supremacists) and counter-protesters advocating for human rights at a Unite the Right Rally in Charlottesville, Virginia, in August 2017, President Trump stated, "there were difficulties and misbehavior from both sides." President Trump was also famously quoted as saying there were "many fine people on both sides." We've all seen the photos from that rally of the White Nationalists. I am willing to bet that you can remember those images without having to look them up. The hundreds of burning torches look like a reincarnation of the Klu Klux Klan. There is no mistaking what is motivating the screaming crowd; it can be seen all too plainly on the faces of these young men: a doctrine based on hate, oppression, subjugation, *"we are better than"*, a return to white supremacy, and several of the symbols and slogans of the Nazi regime. The President, who is arguably the single most powerful person in the world, sets an incredibly important example of how to embrace responsibility, Internal Accountability, and civility—or not.

Just before this book was published, Trump was quoted as saying that the Black Lives Matter organization is a "symbol of racism," in sharp contrast with his complimentary description of white supremist hate groups. Lastly, the first televised presidential debate with former Vice President Joseph Biden took place on September 29, 2020. Trump was pressed by moderator Chris Wallace to answer the question "Are you willing, tonight, to condemn white supremacists and militia groups, and, to say they need to stand down and not add to the violence in a number of these cities, as we saw in Kenosha and Portland?" Trump once again deflected the question, and was pressed by the moderator again.

Trump struggled for a few moments and appeared taken aback. I could help but think this is what happens to a schoolyard bully when someone stands up to them. Trump soon regrouped and started badgering the moderator, and he started building up steam: "You want to call them... what do you want to call them? Give me a name, give me a name—go ahead, who would you like me to condemn? Who?" The former Vice President said a specific name of a white hate group two times. Trump's response to the referenced hate group: "stand back and stand by," followed by, "But I'll tell you what, I'll tell you what... somebody has got to do something about Antifa and the Left." There is no question about who our current President is and what he stands for.

I believe that eventually "people leak out" no matter how hard they try to keep their true nature, or perhaps their dominant parts, behind the dam. I believe that Trump's true nature didn't just leak out during that debate—it gushed. When he would not "condemn" the violence and actions of white hate groups, he emboldened those very organizations whose mission is to violate the tenets and principles of Dignity and Respect for *all* people. He sent a wave—perhaps a tsunami—to empower those whose purpose is to *increase* the divide in an effort to fully restore systemic oppression.

And he even provided their rallying cry.

Even more egregious, (if that is even possible) on a national level, than his support of hate groups has been his abysmal response to the COVID-19 pandemic. When it struck, President Trump discussed how the Center for Disease Control (CDC) has recommended that people start wearing masks to slow down the spread of the virus. President Trump said, "I don't think I'm going to be doing it." Incredibly, and I don't use that word in a positive way, he commented, "I just don't want to be doing-somehow sitting in the Oval Office behind that beautiful Resolute Desk, the great Resolute Desk, I think wearing a face mask as I greet presidents, prime ministers, dictators, kings, queens. I don't know, somehow I don't see it for myself. Maybe I'll change my mind, but this will pass, and hopefully it will pass very quickly."

As of October 2020, more than 200,000 human beings have died in the United States related to the COVID-19 virus; more than 7 million have been infected; it has cost the country, and you and me, trillions of dollars. Who knows how much better our situation could have been had President Trump set a more responsible example and put the health of American citizens above petty vanity?

Through the lens of responsibility, accountability, civility, and leadership, President Trump continues to fall staggeringly short of the mark.

Obedience to Authority

There are many who would argue that the behavior of a person in power has no real bearing on the decisions and values of individuals—that our morals and ethics remain intact despite what happens "at the top." These people are clearly ignoring history.

In 1961, Stanley Milgram, Ph.D., a psychologist at Yale, conducted a series of social experiments to explore the relationship between obedience and authority. He suggested that the concept of obedience—often considered a virtue—may help explain why there was such a level of compliance by German citizens and soldiers in the annihilation of the Jewish population. He investigated what happens when a human being is faced with "the moral question of whether one should obey when commands conflict with conscience." (Obedience to Authority, p 2).

Milgram posited that the presence of an authority figure could facilitate a *shift* from a person's previously held moral standard, to one whereby a person is willing to inflict harm and/or punishment on another person. In addition, he also wanted to investigate how the subjects in the experiment would explain *why* they were willing and/or compelled to do so. A person's internal and external sense of accountability and responsibility became a significant predictor in this world-renowned study, which has been replicated hundreds of times, with similar results and conclusions.

Furthermore, as a process of obeying, a person may feel less, or no longer, responsible for their actions. Once this displacement of responsibility occurs—and it can happen in an incredibly short period of time—

there is a significant alteration in a person's ability to adhere to their previously held moral compass. I believe the IFS model and mechanisms such as rationalization, justification, and blame can provide explanations as to why a person could be so readily influenced and compelled.

Milgram and his team advertised for volunteers to participate in a study of memory and learning. Unbeknownst to the volunteers, Milgram's experiment has nothing to do with what they are told. The experiment is really to explore the degree to which a normal person would punish and inflict pain on another human being, especially when prompted by an authority figure.

The experiment involved three people—two volunteers and one experimenter. The experimenter is the one running the experiment in the psychology lab. The volunteers who answered the advertisement are assigned to be the "teachers" and the "learners". But it's a *rigged* process. Unbeknownst to the volunteer designated as the teacher, the "learner" and the "experimenter"(who serves as the authority figure), are part of Milgram's team and follow scripted roles, depending on the behavior of the teacher. Once in the laboratory, the volunteer/teacher is told the "study is concerned with the effects of punishment on learning." (p.3) (Milgram has been criticized for this "bait and switch" dynamic. I don't know how he would have otherwize undertaken this groundbreaking study. If he advertised for people who were willing to hurt other human beings, he probably would not have been able to extrapolate his groundbreaking conclusions!)

The volunteer/teacher is told the learner's task is to memorize word pairs, and for every incorrect answer the teacher will administer an electric shock which will increase in intensity with each wrong answer. The learner is placed in a room and sits in a chair, has his arms strapped down on the arm rests, and a wire and electrode is affixed to his wrist. The learner will never be shocked during the experiment, but will react like he is.

In addition, the shocks the volunteer/teacher thought they were administering in the Milgram experiments were through a "shock generator" that looked very real and imposing. The alleged shocks were administered by turning a dial that was clearly labeled in gradations from Slight Shock (the lowest voltage) to Danger: Severe Shock.

To help convince the volunteer/teacher they would be administering actual electricity to the learner, the experimenter would administer a real, and very small shock (45 volts) to the teacher. Once the experiment started the learner would soon answer a question incorrectly.

For every alleged wrong answer, the experimenter instructed the teacher to shock the learner with an incrementally higher voltage. The supposed voltage started at approximately 15 volts. At 75 volts, the learner would issue a grunt; at 150 volts the learner is vocal and adamant to stop the experiment; and at 285 volts the learner responds with screams of agony, and acting as if they were being electrocuted.

If the teacher hesitated or resisted shocking the learner, the experimenter would give one of four verbal prods, of increasing intensity, to continue the experiment:

Please continue.
The experiment requires that you continue.
It is absolutely essential that you continue.
You have no other choice; you must go on. (p.21)

Although I guess the experiments could have been terminated by a teacher running out of the building, this did not appear to have happened. Instead the experiment would stop under the following conditions:

1) If the teacher refused to continue shocking the learner after four verbal prods.
2) If the teacher "had" shocked the learner three times in a row, with the highest voltage possible (450 volts).

Milgram elaborated two theories on why the subjects/teachers were willing to shock the learner:

1) Theory of conformism, which proposes that being in a group shifts the frame of reference for an individual. Conformity suggests an individual will defer to a group hierarchy, especially if that individual lacks confidence and expertise in the given situation.

2) The Agentic State Theory, which more closely intercepts with the themes in this book. This theory postulates that because of the phenomenon and effect of obedience to an authority figure, an individual is no longer guided by an internal sense of responsibility and accountability, and perceives someone or something else as responsible for their own behavior. Dr. Milgram expounds that a shift has occurred for a person in the Agentic State, "from their former self." *p 143* (Note Dr. Milgram's use of the word *self*.)

While Dr. Milgram's explanation is fairly complex, as Michael Elkin states, "IFS can make the complex simple, and the simple complex." From an IFS perspective, we can describe the Agentic State as "simply" being manipulated away from Self-leadership and into a part-led system.

Once we have been shifted into a part-led system in this type of environment, several Cognitive Physio Mechanisms will be utilized to protect and/or shield the parts from the impact and consequences of our/their actions. This is true during, and especially *after,* administering the alleged electrical shocks. To his credit, at the conclusion of each experiment, Dr. Milgram and his team explained in detail the real focus of the teacher's role, and also had them meet and talk with the learner to assure them they were not harmed in any way. But I wonder about the effects on the volunteers many years later.

Dr. Milgram classified subjects who participated in the study into 3 categories:

1) Obeyed (the authority figure) but justified themselves
2) Obeyed but blamed themselves
3) Rebelled
4) Obeyed but justified themselves

Explained through a lens of IFS and Cognitive Physio Mechanisms (CPMs), participants who followed the prompts from the authority figure shifted their personal responsibility and accountability from an internal locus of control to an external locus: i.e. what happened was the responsibility of the authority figure and/or the learner. Within an IFS framework, we would conceptualize this as a *part* succumbing to an outside influence, and CPMs such as rationalization, justification, and blame also coming into play. For instance, in this category a familiar explanation by the volunteer/teacher was to blame the experimenter for their behaviors. One volunteer/teacher said outright that it was the experimenter's fault for what had happened or could happen to the learner. Another familiar scenario in this category was to blame the learner in order to justify their behavior. One teacher described the learner as, "so stupid and stubborn he deserved to be shocked."

Obeyed but Blamed Themselves

Explained through the lens of IFS and Cognitive Physio Mechanisms, participants in this category had an internal critic/part, which would demean the "teacher/subject" because they thought they were inflicting pain on the learner and did not adequately resist the instructions of the experimenter. I would imagine if the teachers were questioned, they would likely feel Shame. As Mike Elkin said, "Shame is your badness being witnessed."

Rebelled

Not that I am in the same planetary system as Dr. Milgram, but I respectfully suggest that a more descriptive name for this category could be *Resisted*.

Explained through the lens of IFS and CPMs, participants who rebelled/resisted (were unwilling to continue) had a critical mass of Self and were not as likely to administer ever-increasing shocks to the learner. The participants who were in this category also were able to challenge the authority figure and referred to universal truths such as an internal sense of accountability/responsibility, morals, and ethics. (Note: these are my interpretations).

Eventually, the subjects in this category—as Dr. Milgram noted—rebelled and did not continue. However, to my knowledge all participants in the numerous studies administered some level of what they believed was an electric shock. That is why I used the word resisted.

This is a very important distinction because in the literature of torture there is something called "aquiescing to trivial demands." This is a sequential strategy/technique with the intent of ultimately compromising a person's moral compass and altering their sense of responsibility and accountability. The framework is to start by eliciting a response to a series of non-threatening questions and/or required behaviors. These initial questions and behaviors are specifically designed to not significantly challenge a person's inner moral compass. However, the intent is to move up the ladder to incrementally compromise a person's sense of responsibility and moral beliefs to eventually elicit significant disclosures and harmful behaviors. This process is instituted in stages and is fully delineated in what is widely known as the CIA's manual of torture: *The KUBARK Counterintelligence Interrogation Manual*, which was declassified and obtained by me to use in trainings I conducted on the parallels of torture and domestic violence.

What was not predicted by Milgram, social scientists, or participants, was the level of compliance of the test subjects—and more importantly, their willingness to inflict what they believed to be high voltage shocks. In one experimental trial, over 60 percent of teachers/subjects administered the 450 volt shock. It was also established in **every** experimental trial that **all** the "teachers" shocked the "learner" at a lower level.

To put this amount of voltage into context, your regular house current is 120 volts. If you have ever tried to change a light switch without shutting off the power, and got a shock, once is enough! 240 volts is enough to electrocute someone immediately. A 450 volt shock would literally fry a person where they stand.

So, a short story from my band days to put voltage in perspective: When we would perform at certain concert venues or clubs, we would often need to access their electric panel. Why this dangerous quest? Because we needed the club's/venue's 240 volt circuits to power our sound system. Most circuits were 120 volts and would not provide nearly enough current. Our lead singer, Steve Smith, would access the electric panel, take the cover off, then unscrew the 240 volt circuit connections with a very large mechanic's screwdriver. One evening he was connecting our power lines to the circuit board at a club called the Engine Company when he inadvertently

What Can Erode a Sense of Responsibility, Accountability, and Civility?

made contact with the live wire and the ground wire with the shaft of the screwdriver. When this happened there was a "ZZZZZZZZZTTT!!!!!!!" that sounded like a lightning bolt, and a weird acrid smoke odor. Steve went flying backwards across the basement floor like he was shot out of a cannon. I will never forget my amazement that Steve was still alive. I was also amazed that the thick screwdriver was smoking and almost sliced in half like it was cut by a laser beam. That's "just" a 240 volt system.

Critics of the Milgram experiment may say the average person is not familiar with what constitutes a "merely" painful shock as compared to a life-threatening one. However, this argument does not hold up, given that the actors that were supposedly being shocked would yell, scream, plead, beg the "teacher" to stop, and be heard writhing in their chair as a result of the shock.

Milgram came to a conclusion and extrapolated that one of the main components of obedience occurs when a person feels, thinks, or believes another person or group is *responsible* for their behavior. I believe Dr. Milgram's experiments, though they may not account for all diversions from responsibility and accountability, reveal an essential framework for families, governments, religions, and cultures, which oppress and subjugate their members in some way. But just like in yin and yang—there is a light in this darkness. When the teachers who stopped "shocking" the actors were asked why they refused to continue administering electric shocks, their answer was because "they felt responsible for their behavior no matter what the authority figure directed them to do." (*Obedience to Authority*, Milgram 1974).

There is an additional component to be extrapolated from this groundbreaking experiment: how easily empathy and compassion can be manipulated and eroded. We are born with the hardware and wiring for empathy—and more specifically, compassion—although this potential lies dormant at birth. But because empathy and compassion are universal truths, they can develop over time, even in the harshest of environments. However, Milgram's experiments—which have been replicated many times—clearly demonstrate that it doesn't take a rocket scientist to figure out how to shift people's sense of empathy, compassion, responsibility, and accountability. It's actually a straightforward and well-defined framework and process. Furthermore, given the "right" circumstances, we *all* can be susceptible to it. The prompts instructing the teachers to inflict pain were verbal and rather benign compared to what human beings are capable of and do. As Gavin de Becker once told me, "If you can think of it, it's already been done."

That is why it is *so* important to choose our leaders well.

The Power and Harm of Shame

If you are curious why we *all* abdicate responsibility at one time or another, we need to explore the role of shame as a major reason. As Michael Elkin, LMFT states in Appendix B: "Shame is your badness witnessed by others." and "Shame is so painful we would often endure physical pain rather than the psychological and emotional experience of being a shameful human being." Experiencing shame can be intolerable to our internal system. Thus our Managers, and especially our Firefighters, will do anything to avoid feeling Shame, regardless of the consequences. And universal truths such as responsibility, accountability, and civility, can fall by the wayside.

In an effort to bridge the gap that can happen when we assume someone interprets a word the same way we would, I have included definitions of both Shame and guilt, given how they are often thought to be somewhat interchangeable. This next section will explore how they are quite different.

Helen Block Lewis distinguishes shame from guilt. She posits the major difference between the two is that: "shame is about the self." We say, "I am ashamed of *myself*," as compared to guilt which is, "I am guilty *for* something." Guilt is out there in the real world, something you did or something you thought that you shouldn't have thought."

In addition, while shame is an incredibly powerful internal experience, it also extends to the larger (macro) systems of our life. While there are too many scenarios to include in this chapter, let's look at one brief example of shame's potential impact, from one of the most respected organizations in the world.

The Harvard Negotiation Project (HNP), which we will explore further in Chapter 11, is a distinguished center for the study of negotiation,

What Can Erode a Sense of Responsibility, Accountability, and Civility?

and the successful resolution of conflict. A critical aspect of their research is the importance of being internally and externally accountable to the person, group, and/or country you are negotiating with. The authors are clear: successful negotiations are governed by *respectful* interactions. It is my extrapolation—but I am confident the HNP members will agree—that shaming the other person or group is not an aspect of their model, and is the very thing **not to do**. The HNP emphasises the *process* of *how* we negotiate is as important as the actual outcome. Trust is a necessary component of negotiations at the highest level, and in families as well. Inherent in these interactions is the ability to listen, to be responsible, to be accountable, and to be civil—even when the heat gets turned up. Conversely, without these attributes the entire process is derailed. When the proverbial train goes off the tracks, the stage is now set—actually, a battlefield of sorts—where the diminishment or absence of personal responsibility, accountability, and civility, lead to increasing rigidity, escalation, us vs. them mentality, systemic and entrenched positions, and ever-increasing conflict. Unfortunately, this is our current political model on both sides of the aisle, often fueled by the media, and is President Trump's model as well. And it's not a cautionary tale—it is happening as we speak.

Our internal system can experience the same type of derailment when we make a responsible choice, but if it was/is predicated on Shame, we seldom reap the benefits. Why? Because the "core fuel" of Shame is that we are less than, defective, worthless, reprehensible, irredeemable, dirty, etc. So despite what you do in your life, you *are* still those things—regardless of your deeds. Even more importantly, shame can obscure the universal truth that you don't have to *do* or *be* anything to be worthwhile—*you are inherently* worthwhile as a human being. When Shame drives a choice, we are left with yet another confirmation of hopelessness, because at the end of the day we are still immutably defective.

Ann Sinko, LMFT has a very helpful guide to how our Managers believe they are preventing and protecting us from experiencing Shame.

The Rules of Shame = The Managers Creed
Manager parts live by the motto: "Never Again"

1) **Control:** Be in control of all behaviors and interactions—both yours and everyone else's.
2) **Perfection:** Always be "right,"—do the right thing, strive for perfection, and use criticism to try to ensure perfection.
3) **Blame:** If something does not happen as you plan, or if you feel something you don't want to feel, blame (self or others).
4) **Denial:** Deny feelings, especially negative or vulnerable ones.
5) **Unreliability:** Do not expect reliability or constancy in relationships. Watch for the unpredictable. DO NOT TRUST!
6) **Incompleteness:** Don't bring transactions to resolution or completion because you might have to face feelings or honest revelations you're protecting against. Don't let secrets out.
7) **No Talk:** Don't talk openly and directly about shameful, abusive, or compulsive behaviors or feelings.
8) **Disqualification:** When disrespectful, shameful, abusive, or compulsive behaviors occur, disqualify, deny, or disguise them. Make excuses.

Reprinted by permission, Ann Sinko. Adapted from Evan Imber-Black's Rules of Shame from Secrets in Families and Family Therapy *(1993, p 37)*

Michael Elkin has written a beautiful protocol to conceptualize and address the negative effects of chronic/intense Shame, especially when it is experienced/perceived as insurmountable. When we are burdened by the unrelenting experience of Shame, sometimes the only course left, seemingly, is to give up hope. Michael has written and addressed this phenomenon in his Despair Protocol. He states, "When a person has suffered the pain of disappointment and the shame of failure—the only thing left, the only instrumentality that is available to a person, is to give up trying." (The Despair Protocol, Michael Elkin)

Once a person gives up trying, they can, paradoxically, regain a sense of autonomy and instrumentality. However, there is a great price to pay for this reprieve as a person's internal system now resides in a state of perpetual helplessness—and opportunities to remediate the shame are actually experienced as a threat and rejected—because giving up hope is significantly less painful than endless experiences of disappointment and failure. In Elkin's protocol, the Exile that carries the burden of shame and hopelessness is viewed as doing the best it could under the circumstances. Critical in Elkin's model, is to express to the person's internal system that it could not have possibly known at the time that there would be other resources available—to and for it—in the future.

Shame is so damaging because it is often experienced as immutable. In my view, guilt is experienced as something **you can atone** or make amends for.

Shame is experienced as something **you are,** with no redemption possible; and/or you are what you have done, or what has happened to you. Acknowledging the importance and role of Shame is a necessary component of understanding the contextual framework when exploring how, when, and where we embrace universal truths, and when we do not.

The Development of Empathy and Compassion

On a lighter note, let me relay another anecdote—this one about Emily, our middle daughter. Emily was about 5 years old and playing with her younger sister, Christina. At one point Emily picked up a wiffle ball bat and started to tap her sister with it. This was not one of those soft oversized wiffle ball bats; it was one of those narrow, very hard plastic ones, made for really sending the ball quite a far distance. Eventually, Emily started hitting Christina more forcefully; Christina started crying, and I ran into the room to intervene. I said something perfunctory like, "Emily stop hitting your sister right now." And let me add this was one of my better days of parenting; I didn't yell, speak harshly, or intimidate by using my size. (I've done all the above at one time or another.) Emily stopped and just looked at me with her big brown eyes. I said more sharply, "Did you hear me?!" Then, Emily, to the envy of every Samurai warrior, took that bat, swung it in a perfect arc, and struck me square in the forehead with all her might. I must admit I saw some stars and white spots, but as I said, this was one of my better days of parenting. Although my brain felt more than a little scrambled, I managed, "Emily, that really hurt Daddy." And Emily looked at me with those big brown eyes and said, *"But it didn't hurt me."* I knew that if I was not concussed and able to remember this exchange I would be telling it for years to come. Well, Emily is now 20, so I guess I retained enough of my short term memory.

Why this story? Because empathy and compassion are something that we, as human beings, develop over time. They are essential components of feeling and being connected to others. A famous psychoanalyst, Heiz Kohut, postulated that "a sense of self" (Kohut used this term well before IFS was developed) is formed in part by a level of narcissism. Kohut coined the term "healthy narcissism," as a normal developmental stage of children. For instance, think of the last time your child sat down with you, at somewhere between 5-12 years old, and said: "Hey, enough about me! I just want to sit here and hear all about your day. Take your time, I cleared my next two hours." That is just not something we, as parents, are used to!

If we were to put it in clinical terms we would describe that as a "parentified child." What we do (ideally) as parents, teachers, coaches, and mentors is teach our children that other people's feelings and wellbeing matter and are important, often with a version of, "Do unto others...," the kid version being: "Would you like it if someone did that to you?" The point is that it is a process. It is not surprising then that the standard framework to establish oppressive regimes is to start with the children. Children are particularly vulnerable because they are dependent on adults, do not have a well-established moral compass, and are narcissistic at this developmental stage. History has shown us this. It's as if there is a dark instructional manual on how to erode empathy and compassion, and objectify human beings, and it capitalizes on children's dependency and pliability. Hitler and the Nazi regime did this by indoctronation through the Hitler youth organization; Pol Pot did it by kidnapping and enslaving children and then requiring them to serve in the army. The military regime of Rwanda did a similar thing by murdering parents, kidnapping their children, and conscripting them to become child soldiers, who were often refered to as *kadogo* or "little ones" in Kiswahili. In our own country we justified the genocide of Indigenous people, and inculcated the "normalcy" of kidnapping and enslavement of Africans.

Empathy is defined by the American Heritage Dictionary as "understanding so intimately that the feelings, thoughts, and motives of one are readily comprehended by another." Webster's definition is "the action of understanding, being aware of, being sensitive to, and vicariously experiencing the feeling, thought, and experience" of another. Empathy is often described as seeing the world through another's eyes, walking a mile in their shoes, etc. It is incredibly easy to diminish empathy for others. Seen through the lens of IFS, Dr. Milgram's research, and Cognitive Physio Mechanisms, once the dimension of empathy and compassion has been diminished, a framework can be established—neurologically, culturally, and systemically—to experience another human being as *the other*. At that juncture, the path has been cleared for someone or something to become *less than*.

As briefly illuminated in Chapter 1, we only need to look as far as our own Declaration of Independence to witness the power of these dimensions. The Declaration of Independence is often referred to as one of the greatest documents ever written and has been a foundation of the United States of America's history and influence. Yet, the foundational passage, "We hold these truths to be self-evident" precedes "all men are created equal." Codified in our great country's document is that word "men." Certainly it is a reflection of the times, but it also illuminates how even such an important document can also legitimize and codify that women are not equal to men. This did not work out well for women then, and we as a society are still feeling the effects in the present. And what about the human beings kidnapped from their home and country—enslaved, tortured, raped, oppressed, or killed to build and grow the colonies and then the country? The word "men" did not include the males among these enslaved human beings, and women were of even lower status, if that is even possible given the level of degradation. But as we have explored, the framework of Milgram experiments, Cognitive Physio Mechanisms, the developmental course of empathy, the imbalance of a parts-led system, and the erosion of empathy fulfill all the structural requirements for oppression, subjugation, and enslavement.

There were some people who realized the incongruent nature of the words "all men are created equal." In 1776, abolitionist Thomas Day wrote: "If there be an object truly ridiculous in nature, it is an American patriot, signing resolutions of independencey with the one hand, and with the other brandishing a whip over his affrighted slaves." (Armitage,

David. *The Declaration of Independence: A Global History.* 76-77/ Cambridge, Massachusetts: Harvard University Press, 2007.)

Systematic and Systemic Oppression

The alchemy of oppression includes utilizing a distorted version of universal truths (such as responsibility, accountability, and civility), to continue to oppress and subjugate the identified group. For instance, if we believe that slaves, Africans, and blacks are a lesser form of life, we can be said to have a *responsibility* to keep them in their place—and we are *accountable* as good citizens to keep from believing they are worthwhile. We can embrace being civil, but being *civil* doesn't apply to them, because they are less than us. We will develop laws that govern how to obtain, buy, and sell this property, without any restrictions on how we treat "them" because they are less than us.

Once a group has been codified as *less than*, especially in terms of not having the right to vote or run for office, it assures the disenfranchised group will encounter incredible levels of oppression and spend many years in the quest—really, the fight—for some semblance of human rights.

The same has been true in the oppression of women. Women's quest for equal rights and the right to vote began in the 1800s and was fraught with danger, oppression, systematic genderism, and harm. It wasn't until 1878 when an amendment was presented to the House of Representatives to establish women's right to vote. It was not ratified at that time and took until May 21, 1919 to be passed by the House. Soon after it was passed by the Senate. Still, three-fourths of the states were needed to support the amendment. Finally, it was ratified by the state of Tennessee on August 18, 1920. Our Declaration of Independence paradoxically codified and institutionalized the systemic oppression of women. It would take over *one hundred and forty-four years* before the 19th Amendment was ratified to law. And even once it was, in practice the right to vote still did not extend to *all* women.

Many of the effects of what was systematically institutionalized hundreds of years ago—for blacks and for women—continue to this day. As

Ann Sinko describes in Appendix B, legacy burdens carry great importance, impact, and power. The only hopeful path for change is to fully recognize and unburden them (as much as is possible). This path will be a challenging one at best. If we undertake an effort to repair the legacy burdens of the past, *how* we treat each other during the process is equally important to achieving *what* we set out to accomplish.

Revisionist History

Last, but certainly not least in this chapter is the reality and effect that revisionist history has on the erosion of responsibility, accountability, and civility. Revisionist history occurs when the facts of a historical event or events have been altered, misrepresented, or misinterpreted over time, and is no longer a factual recounting of what happened. There is almost always a group who benefits in some way from this revision.

For an example, look no further than Columbus Day, celebrated in October as the day Christopher Columbus "discovered" America (nevermind that he actually landed on an island in what is now the Bahamas). What a wonderful day off of work for most of us! However, how could a person *discover* a continent when there were already people living there? Indigenous people, Native Americans, had already been living on this continent long before Columbus arrived, with their own histories, legacies, social structures, tribes, lands, customs, families, and governments. Most indigenous cultures were decimated, plundered, and enslaved as Columbus and other European explorers sailed to the "New World." Columbus didn't discover our continent, but this holiday continues to be observed hundreds of years later. This is an example of Revisionist history, still "celebrated" to this day in many states. Some progressive states such as South Dakota, Alaska, New Mexico, Maine, and Vermont have recognized this injustice and alteration of our history and have supplanted Columbus Day with Indigenous People's Day.

In the following month we've got Thanksgiving—more Revisionist history of how the pilgrims and settlers populated what was known as the new land. I remember watching Westerns with my father, and in all the movies and TV shows at the time, Indigenous people—labeled Injuns, or Indians—were portrayed as savages: not too bright, yelling, screaming, and killing innocent women and children. What was not portrayed at that time was the reality of the Native American experience. That movie or TV show would show how over time, the people who came to this continent stole the indigeouos peoples land, took over their resources, murdered many of their people, began the macro process of genocide, and raped, enslaved, and objectified the race and culture into something *less than* human. On top of that, for hundreds of years, the charming story of the "First Thanksgiving" would be taught to young children as history.

Once Revisionist history has been established, it facilitates denial, justification, the erosion of compassion, and institutionalized oppression. The destruction of the very foundation and fabric of a people and culture results in a self-perpetuating mechanism that blames the very people who were—and continue to be—oppressed. Then, it's "their" fault that "they" cannot return to former prosperity, or take advantage of the opportunities available now. When empathy and compassion are eroded, it becomes rather easy to blame a culture for their disenfranchised position in life. And the oppressors never need to grapple with the real causes.

The effects of the enslavement of Africans in America have rippled through the Black community, and our nation's history, for centuries. How does the revision continue to perpetuate? Once Revisionist history has been recalibrated, it often is sustained by mechanisms such as rationalization. For example, folks may acknowledge the horrific history of enslavement, but with the "aid" of rationalization it might sound like this:

"Well, yes, 'they' were stolen from their country and enslaved, but that was hundreds of years ago. But now 'they' are free. *Everybody* can get ahead in America. This is the land of prosperity. Time for *them* to pick *themselves* up and get to work!"

Therefore, through a distorted socratic logic lens, if a group or culture cannot get ahead now, it must be their fault—their laziness, their inherent defectiveness, etc. Revisionist history is particularly difficult to address because the causal linkage to what has happened before has been severed, and the origins became seemingly unrelated to the present day. The great paradox is that the solution to those injustices (to whatever level is possible), requires revisiting and revising the Revisionist history itself.

But it can be incredibly difficult to do, because the structure of Revisionist history erodes our capacity for empathy (identifying *with*) and compassion (doing something *for*) and distorts these qualities over time. Aspects of empathy, and especially compassion (which I believe are part of our essence), when not Self-led, can actually sustain Revisionist history! Once the past is rewritten, it sets the foundation and framework for another self-perpetuating mechanism—which can make it *seem* like we experience empathy and compassion, but it is actually designed to facilitate a distorted version of these characteristics.

For example, if we feel empathy towards someone or something, we can identify *with* instead of doing something *about* or *for*. "Oh that poor homeless person, that poor drug addict, that poor child, it's so, so sad." Empathy can shift seductively into pity. Pity can be especially tolerated because its framework still allows us to feel sorry for, and identify *with* a person, group, or culture, but it also includes a level of disgust and/or repulsion towards that group. For instance, "Oh, that poor homeless person, it's so sad, I'm so glad that's not me, they're gross." "Oh, that drug addict, what a horrible addiction, that's what happens when you look for the easy way out."

Even compassion can be compromised. It can sound like, "Hey, we spent millions of dollars on No Child Left Behind, Just say No, and *they* are still not doing what *they* need to do. We are helping *them*, but they are not taking advantage of our programs, generosity, and funding." But these things do nothing to address the origin, foundation, and legacy of a disenfranchised group. If this effort to "help" does not address and remediate the *historical* harm incurred (to whatever extent is possible), these programs and efforts are usually an exercise in futility. The end product encodes a distorted sense of empathy and compassion; we can still maintain we've done something *for them*, but *they* haven't succeeded despite all the opportunities, and so it's still *their* fault. The "best" of both worlds for systematic and institutional oppression.

Just as I was finishing writing this book, two horrific events took place in the United States. A young man, Ahmaud Arbery, was accosted by a father, Gregory McMichael, who was armed with a pistol and his son, Travis, who was armed with a shotgun. Both McMichaels ambushed Mr. Arbery while he was jogging, and Travis McMichael shot and killed Arbery with a shotgun. Mr. Arbery, who was unarmed, was murdered. However, that did not stop Gregory McMichael from attempting to create his own revisionist history to blame Mr. Arbery because "he believed he resembled the suspect in a series of local break-ins." (BBC NEWS May 08, 2020). This murder is absolutely a reflection of racism in our country, which has its roots in the Revisionist history generated to protect me, maybe you, from the realities of what happened hundreds of years ago. I believe that Revisionist history was an integral aspect of why it took more than two months for the McMichaels to be charged with the crime.

Ramifications of Forgetting the Past

This all paints a rather bleak picture. So are we as human beings, at our essence, good? My esteemed teachers and mentors believe so. As Mike Elkin, LMFT says in his in Appendix B, "Dick believes that, and I do not know that to be not true." This could be an endless debate. So, I will weigh in. Like Michael, I don't know that to be not true. It is entirely possible that at our core, we are good. However, for whatever reasons, throughout history, human beings have harmed other human beings, at times in the most horrific ways imaginable. If we forget history, or possibly even more harmfully, revise it, we will—as the saying goes—be *doomed to repeat it.*

In the preface to the new edition of *Night*, Elie Wiesel tells a story—actually, a universal truth—of how people, governments, regimes, and unfortunately responsibility itself, can be utilized by people to both bind us and crush the human spirit.

Mr. Wiesel writes of the night of his father's death at the hands of an S.S. officer in a concentration camp they were in together. His father, being beaten with a club as he lies on the floor, calls to him.

What Can Erode a Sense of Responsibility, Accountability, and Civility?

"It had been his last wish to have me next to him in his agony, at the moment when his soul was tearing itself from his lacerated body—yet I did not let him have his wish. I was afraid." (p xi)

"Instead of sacrificing my miserable life and rushing to his side, taking his hand, reassuring him, showing him that he was not abandoned, that I was near him, [and] that I felt his sorrow, instead of all that—I remained flat on my back, asking God to make my father stop calling my name, to make him stop crying. So afraid was I to incur the wrath of the SS." (p. xi)

The young Weisel hears his father's dying words begging him to come close, but he is too scared to move. He will never forgive himself. Mr. Wiesel continues:

"Nor shall I ever forgive the world for having pushed me against the wall, for having turned me into a stranger, for having awakened in me the basest, most primitive instincts. (p. xii)

"His last word had been my name. A summons. And I had not responded." (p. xii)

Elie Weisel carried with him the unimaginable burdens of Holocaust, and of his father's death, and feels this Shame at the most profound level, to the very core of who he is. When a victim—in this warped framework of oppression and subjugation—believes they are in some way responsible for what has happened to them or to someone else at the hands of an oppressor, the oppressor has succeeded in infusing an unfathomable level of shame and despair into the victim. In Mr. Wiezel's example, *he*, not the Nazi regime, was to blame for his father's agony.

This paradigm is what I previously referenced as the dark instruction manual. It is mirrored in racism, domestic violence/abuse, misogyny, genderism, etc. The way these experiences are encoded, embodied, and experienced cannot be addressed through an intellectual exercise. But there is hope.

PART VI

THE FUTURE

CHAPTER 11

HOPE
&
*The Principle of Responsibility
and Civility Redefined*

The Internal Family System paradigm can offer a foundation, framework, and path to healing and hope. However, there are other paths, and I do not believe Internal Family Systems is the only one. What I have come to believe—to actually have full conviction of—is that because IFS is both a psychotherapy model *and* a model for living our lives, it offers a firm foundation and framework for the many of the topics we are exploring together.

I have continued to use several stories about my experiences as a clinical social worker and family life—not because I am trying to impress you, or suggest we are in some way self actualized. The opposite is in fact true. Like Arron Beck has said, people are not swayed by the number of counter arguments—they are swayed by something that makes sense to them. These experiences, and others, have made sense to me. I invite you to look at these sections, if not through the lens of IFS, then whatever lens, story, or path resonates with you. Explore what makes sense *to you*.

Here we go...

Vote

There are many things that have always *been* great about our country, and one of the most important and critical aspects of our nation's resilience is that we have the ability to cast a vote for those we choose to represent us. In so many areas and countries in the world, the opportunity to have any input in your own government is not remotely available. In fact, to say or write something negative about your government, or to advocate for the right to vote could mean you or your family will be incarcerated, tortured, or murdered.

We *can* vote for who we choose to represent us. I don't believe voting is necessarily a right like a universal truth, but I totally believe it is a *privilege* and a *gift*. Unfortunately, in the last presidential election, as in many others, only about fifty-five percent of eligible Americans voted for who they wanted to represent us. The other forty-five percent represents about *one-hundred million* people who did not vote! Rather than see that number through the lens of blame and judgment, I see it as an opportunity. Imagine if just a fraction of those Americans enter that voting booth with fresh eyes attuned to the world we want to build, and the values we want to establish for future generations.

I hope the examples and stories in this book help with how we choose who represent us, what they stand for, and whether they demonstrate responsibility, accountability, and civility. Perhaps more importantly, when they falter—and they will because we all do—what happens then? Do they treat people civilly? Do they ever apologize for mistakes? Is it sincere and straightforward, or do they apologize in some convoluted way? These are civil servants, and they answer to us. Not the other way around.

Seeking Help

In my clinical practice, it is not unusual to see a family system whose members do not treat each other well. Parents will often say their children need to treat them with respect, and children usually echo the same sentiments. In such cases, I will define dignity and respect and acknowledge that it's a universal desire to be treated in this manner. Then I will define the most basic definition of being civil (merely refraining from rudeness, being polite in a perfunctory way). It is a painful truth that some families are not ready to treat each other with dignity and respect, and it will be challenging for them to meet even the most rudimentary definition of being civil. For these families, I will suggest we try to work towards being civil to each other—starting in my office. In addition, I will share that they already have an innate ability for compassion, and we will work on developing specific skills over time. Usually at this point someone will say, "So you're saying I have to be civil to them, even when they are not being civil to me? That's not going to work!" This is *not* a huge selling point, at first, for families to begin to trust me; however, my response is, "I know it sounds counterintuitive, but, yes! We will explore and discover why being civil can be so difficult." If there is an extended negotiation about refusing to be civil, I sometimes resort to this exchange (which is a double bind paradigm, I fully acknowledge). Here is an example:

The family and me: We discuss the family dynamics and explore what it would be like to be civil to each other.

PARENT: Well, they will have to be civil to me before I'll be civil to them.

ME: So, before you will be civil they will need to be civil?

PARENT: Right!

ME: And what happens if you think someone is not being civil?

PARENT: Then I'll do what I need to do!

ME: And does that include not being civil?

PARENT: If that's what it takes.

ME: And what happens if you think someone is not being civil and you're mistaken.

PARENT: Well, that's the way it goes…

ME: So you, or a part of you, wants to retain the right to be mean, cruel or even abusive?

PARENT: No, that's not what I said, that's not what I want…

ME: Then what is it you do want?

PARENT: I don't want to be taken advantage of. I want to be listened to.

ME: "Ahhhh… What's really important to you is to be heard and also valued enough to be listened to?"

PARENT: Yes!

ME: So, now we have a starting point. Let's begin. So, how does that sound to everyone else? Pretty reasonable…?

In the beginning of this book, I suggested we could start with being more civil at the most rudimentary level I described. In Dr. Schwartz's interview, he states that when we are able to heal our inner system, by experiencing good "inner parenting," and be in Self, we would naturally treat each other civilly in the way he described. Who's right? Just like the Tai Chi symbol, yin and yang, black and white, soft and strong. Where's the starting point? What's best? We don't have to know. In fact, we can't know what's best because that would mean there is a perfect answer at the end of our inquiry. The quest is what works for you. What many people don't know about the Tai Chi Symbol is it's not a static thing. It represents all the endless permutations of the universe. Just like the ever-present interactions of Self and our parts! How could we ever account for all these permutations? We do not need to. Rather than become mired in where the start point is, history has shown us that we will be unable to move towards something more than 'just' being civil if it does not come from a place, inside of you, that makes sense to do so.

Explore Your Personal History

In IFS we often address what are called legacy heirlooms and legacy burdens (which Ann Sinko, LMFT elaborates on in Appendix B). To illuminate these concepts, specifically legacy heirlooms, in my practice, I tell the following story:

Once upon a time, there was a family preparing for a holiday dinner. Part of their tradition was to make "The Special Ham." Even saying the phrase "The Special Ham" required a deeper voice, and would be like announcing the entrance of a King and Queen. "The Special Ham" was renowned for many generations and required cutting the end off of the ham as part of the preparation. One day, the great great grandchildren asked why the adults cut the end off the ham. Several theories were presented: it allowed the juices to baste the ham from the bottom up, it helped to make it tender, it made the ham cook faster, and so forth. The whole family realized that while the theories sounded plausible, no one really knew. One of the children suggested they ask their Great Great Grandmama who was in the sun room. The children went to the sunroom and asked, and Great Great Grandmama said, "Oh yes, I know why: the pan that my mother used to make the ham was too small, and they were too poor to buy a bigger pan, so she used to cut the end off of it to make it fit. I started doing it because it reminded me of her." This totally made sense to the entire family, and the children discovered something that connected them to five generations. And now, the children's children carry on the tradition and swear it adds to the flavor!

Legacy heirlooms are the traditions, history, values, and ethics that are passed down through generations. They may include such things as ways of expressing love and compassion, honor, responsibility, work ethic, expectations for the future, courage, and cutting the ends off of hams.

> **TO CONSIDER:** What are some of your legacy heirlooms?

DAVID MEDEIROS

Legacy Burdens

Legacy burdens are burdens we carry from past generations. People who have felt the weight of these burdens have sometimes been called, *nuts, crazy, woo woo*. Scientists and trauma theorists have continued to investigate the process of epigenetics, which was conceived in the 1940's by Conrad Waddington, and is a "field of science that studies heritable changes caused by the activation and deactivation of genes without any change in the underlying sequence of the organism." (NIH National Human Genome Research Institute, Laura Elnitski, Ph.D.) Research has continued to expand at an exponential rate, and "Today, a wide variety of illnesses, behaviors, and other health indicators already have some level of evidence linking them with epigenetic mechanisms, including cancers of almost all types, cognitive dysfunction, and respiratory, cardiovascular, reproductive, autoimmune, and neurobehavioral illnesses." (NIH Epigenetics: The Science of Change. Bob Weinhold) In addition, scientists have determined that epigenetic modifications can persist as cells divide, and in some cases passed on to subsequent generations

For example, it is not unfamiliar for children and grandchildren of Holocaust survivors to feel a physical and emotional enervation that does not "make sense" given they have never witnessed the horrors of the Nazi regime directly, and is incongruent with their own life experience. The study of epigenetics is beginning to offer some clues as to why something may be *felt* but not readily explained. We may have not had the words to articulate this state of internal disquiet before, but we are beginning to understand more about how experiences—especially trauma—can be encoded and expressed as *felt* experiences in our physiology: i.e. our brain, mind, body, and gene expression.

TO CONSIDER: Instead of multiple generations growing up being treated and seen as less than, there is a collective and united effort to instill children the building blocks of responsibility and accountability—such as individuals leading by example to treat one another with respect, dignity, and civilly. Can we agree the simple part is the *decision* to start with the children?

Learn to Listen

We have many examples of how to communicate in life. Unfortunately, with the increased visibility and hostility of politicians, reality TV, and talk shows which embrace and encourage conflict and what constitutes "news" in the media, these examples emphasize a communication model that fosters resentment, insults, anger, yelling, threatening, talking over each other, and actual physical attacks. In addition, with the advent of the social media revolution, people can level attacks from afar, with little or no responsibility or accountability for the potential or actual harm caused. It's kind of like being able to lob a hand grenade from a thousand miles away and have perfect accuracy! I am not sure if these politicians, TV shows, and social and news media are a reflection of where we are now as a country, or whether these types of shows and social media have influenced our behavior by normalizing them—probably a combination of both.

Contrast those ways of communicating with examples like that of Bill Miller, Ph.D., the founder of Motivational Interviewing (MI). I had the pleasure of studying with Dr. Miller in New Mexico. I sometimes joke, but it's true—that I traveled all the way to New Mexico to learn how to listen. An essential component of MI is Reflective Listening. In short, Reflective Listening occurs when a person listens to another and is able to reflect the speaker's content back to them in a way that makes the speaker feel heard and understood. In addition, Dr. Miller emphasizes the importance of the listener's ability to reflect the ***emotional*** content of the speaker's message as well. I personally believe that another essential aspect of Reflective Listening is showing the speaker you ***value*** them enough to take the time to reflect back the true essence of what was communicated. Dr. Miller has astutely recognized effective communication is a skill, so he developed a way the listener can quickly check if they really reflected the speaker's content. When the listener has reflected what they thought the speaker means and feels, the listener asks, "Did I get it?" If the speaker can honestly say yes, they have succeeded. If the speaker says no, it is not a failure—because the listener will ask what they missed, and then repeat the process.

I have found IFS to be a huge asset in this skill. When we can be more in Self, we have a much better chance of truly listening and remaining curious, connected, and compassionate. Conversely, when there is an eye roll, a sigh, a body turned away, a dismissive look, or any other bad juju, we can be pretty confident a part has come forward and we probably find that, despite our efforts, it will not go well. Instead of the conversation going to shit at that juncture, utilizing IFS can help us explore what parts may be activated. I can tell you from a personal and professional perspective that Reflective Listening, integrated with IFS, often works out a lot better because most, or all, of our listening skills can go out the window if we are in a part that is supposedly listening, but the intent is to store information for an imminent rebuttal. Let me share an example:

I was working with Joe and Jean, a couple who experienced significant difficulty in many spheres of their lives. They were both vocal about their apprehension of beginning to work with me and afraid this would be just another failed effort. They also told me some of the other therapists they had seen were not too direct with them, and they were looking for someone to be *very* direct. Joe said, "Just tell it to me straight. No Bullshit!"

I recommended we start with Reflective Listening as a communication model. They both said they had practiced this model in previous couple's therapy. I said, "Great!" We reviewed the major tenets of it, and I then asked, "Can you use the Reflective Listening model and discuss what you might be afraid of if this doesn't work out with me?" Jean started first and spoke about all the difficulties they had experienced, and how she really wondered how they would be able to reconnect. Jean shared that just when things started to go well, something would happen, and they would be distant again. She spoke for about 7 minutes during which she was often fighting back tears. When Jean finished I asked Joe if he was ready to reflect on her message. Joe said he was ready and gave an almost word for word description of his wife's talk and incorporated mirroring, repeating, paraphrasing and extrapolating. An impressive display!

He then said to his wife, "Did I get it?"

Jean half heartedly said, "Kind of, mostly."

I looked at Jean and said her responsibility in this exercise was to be as honest as she could be in her response (I had previously investigated if it was safe to do so).

Jean said, "Well…. not really."

Joe looked at me and said, "See, no matter how well I do this, it's not good enough for her!" He then asked me what I thought. Remember, Joseph wanted no BS.

I said, "I think a parrot could have done what you just did." Joseph's jaw dropped. Joe said, "I got everything she said. What's the problem!? A lot of things she said aren't true!" Clearly, Joe was not thrilled.

I said, "I have had many years of practice, and could I try to reflect Jean's talk if that would be helpful."

He said, "Go right ahead."

I looked at Jean and said, "This has been really difficult for you, especially when things are going better and you start to have some hope. But then, something unpleasant happens, and you feel even more distant. If I really try to distill everything you've said, I'd say your heart is broken because you still love him, but it looks like a divorce is the only solution left. Did I get it?"

Here, I was attempting to find the core fuel, the emotional content in what Jean was saying. Well, tears shot out of her eyes, and Jean sobbed for a fair amount of time. We were at the essence and emotional content of what they were both grappling with: hopelessness, despair, grief, and loss. I'm happy to say they worked very hard and they found a way to truly "hear"one another—without the expectation that they must agree—and found so many other seemingly intractable issues could be disentangled. Not everybody makes a reconnection, but they did!

When doing any type of Reflective Listening model, if the emotional essence is not reflected, it often is just a memorization exercise. It won't have the *heart*. What I also let people know is that we often assume listening to a person equates to agreeing with them. I am clear that listening to a person and reflecting their content back does not mean you necessarily agree with them; what it means is that you *value* them enough to openly listen to their point of view and/or experience.

Redefining "The Apology"

In his interview, Dr. Dick Schwartz talked about having the ability to apologize. I believe the apology is one of the most overrated exchanges in our relationship interactions. Think about it, when a person says, "I'm sorry," what are they usually hoping to hear? Often, there is an expectation the person will accept the apology. There can be a sense of relief when the person who says "I'm sorry" hears in response, "That's okay," or even better, "I forgive you." I'm not a big fan of the word forgiveness if the person asking for it is looking to elicit a response that absolves them from responsibility and/or accountability.

Are there exceptions? Of course. As Dr. Schwartz said, "It's important to repair things when your parts take over and do extreme things, and to apologize and take accountability." Now I am not suggesting that a hurt feeling, leaving the toothpaste out, a crass response, or a harsh word requires this level of analysis. Usually an "I'm sorry" between respectful people is more than enough. However, how about if we integrate some of the Principles of Responsibility, accountability and Internal Family Systems for something that warrants a true apology? I support that this type of apology is more like "taking responsibility for," but let's still call it—or label it—an apology. I have a two-tiered template for crafting an apology I find helpful in my personal and professional life.

Tier 1: The Foundation

We would spend time being curious and compassionate towards ourselves and especially others, and internally accountable/answerable for what we did or said. For example, as Dr. Schwartz said, "Yes, I have a part that did that, and I'm going to work with them so they don't keep doing that. But it isn't from a place of, 'I'm a total worthless shit for doing that.'" Then, before we speak, we do an internal scan to request that our parts, if needed, grant us some space so we can deliver the apology with a critical mass of Self and Self-energy. Once we are more confident with Tier 1, we proceed to Tier 2.

Tier 2: The Framework

We would need to acknowledge our mistakes. This usually begins by using the pronoun "I." We use a foundation of responsibility and a framework of Internal Accountability to craft the apology (before we actually do it) instead of asking for forgiveness. What we are saying in the apology must be true.

So here is a respectfully offered template:

> "I want to apologize for _____ but I'm not looking for you to say it's okay, or I forgive you. Rather, I want you to know I've thought a lot about what I've (done, said, did, etc.), and I take responsibility for doing that. I have taken concrete steps to address _____, and I'm more than willing to share them with you if you want, and it's totally understandable if you don't want me to share them with you. I just really wanted you to know. Thanks for listening. Is there anything you want to add?"

I have personally found while this process can seem slow, just like in the practice of drumming or Tai Chi Chuan, sometimes we have to go slower to go faster.

> **TO CONSIDER:** What is your way of apologizing? Does this template seem helpful? If not, what would you change or shift? Reach out to me, I'd love to hear what works for you!

Respectful Communication and Negotiation

The Harvard Negotiation Project is an entity which researches, studies, and teaches how to negotiate on any level—interpersonal, between corporations or governments, and even between countries avoiding war, preparing for war, or engaged in war. They have identified three main frameworks for discussions and negotiations: the Win-Win model, the Win-Lose Model, and the Lose-Lose Model. A Win-Win model is when both sides of the negotiations emerge with a sense of having their needs met in a reasonable way, and a partnership in a shared vision for the future. The authors describe several essential features for a Win-Win outcome:

"To give the other side a feeling of participation, get them involved early. Ask for their advice. Giving credit generously for ideas whenever possible will give them a personal stake in defending those ideas to others. It may be hard to resist the temptation to take credit for yourself, but forbearance pays off handsomely." (p.30 *Getting to YES*)

But perhaps *most* importantly, *how* we come to a decision is an absolutely critical element of whether or not that decision will result in the joining and unifying of the respective parties towards an identified goal. Otherwise, that decision is built on a foundation of sand. The authors write, "Apart from the substantive merits, the feeling of participation in the process is perhaps the single most important factor in determining whether a negotiator accepts a proposal. In a sense, the process *is* the product." (Getting to YES)

A Win-Lose model is one where, instead of a collaborative, respectful, and process oriented goal of a Win-Win model, this paradigm has an undercurrent that the goal really being a sense of power for the "winner" over the "loser" of a contest. When a person, country, or president operates with a Win-Lose model, its framework is *actually to increase* the divisiveness and the division between the respective parties. And, as you can imagine, this does not bode well for future relationships, discussions, and negotiations.

A Lose-Lose model is simply that. Egos dominate the process. Concerns that were once pliable now become intractable. It's us against them. It's like the saying about cutting off your nose off to spite your face, or Trump's Freudian and playground challenge in response to nuclear missile testing by Kim Jong-un of North Korea. "I too have a Nuclear button, but it is a much bigger and more powerful one than his, and my button works."

Talk the Talk and Walk the Walk

As we've seen over and over, being responsible can be a challenging and a potentially unrewarding process. So, a true story about my partner/wife Tricia. Many years ago, Tricia was working at a large consulting firm and had to perform year-end evaluations for her team. The company used several matrices for these evaluations. The most impactful was a scale of performance: Exceptional Performance, Exceeds Expectations, Meets Expectations, Requires Development (in several key areas), and Does Not Meet Expectations. It was not an unfamiliar scenario for employees with the lowest rating to be released (a euphemism for being fired).

One day, an administrator called Tricia before the evaluations were submitted and indicated there were only so many high ratings available for each department. In addition, the administrator said there are "always" people on a team who were not performing, and there was an expectation she would include a certain number of the lowest ratings as well. Tricia stated she did not have employees who fell into the lower rating scale, and that in fact, her team had been working extraordinarily hard, over a long period of time, to deliver several critical applications. The administrator was very clear that some low ratings would have to be given. Tricia knew those low ratings would put her employee's jobs in jeopardy and would not be an accurate reflection of their performance. During subsequent conversations with this administrator, Tricia continued to advocate for her employees and provided substantive information on how most of her team actually met the scale rating of Exceptional Performance or Exceeds Expectations. The administrator was unfazed and reiterated that Tricia needed to revise her evaluations. It was clear the *expectation* was really a *requirement*. This dialogue continued for about two weeks until the administrator told Tricia she must submit the evals that day. Tricia responded, *Since I am unable to revise my employee ratings, I will add myself to the release list.* The administrator was stunned and told her that was not possible. Tricia explained in order to meet the quota, she would consent to be released so her team—who have worked so hard through the year—would not be released. Well, I'm pretty confident the administrator was shocked, as were the people the administrator answered to. However, about two days later, Tricia was given the green light to fairly evaluate her employees and ultimately preserved all of her employee's jobs.

Tricia kept her job as well, but let me be clear: she was not bluffing. You may be thinking this relates to the Obedience to Authority experiments, and you'd be correct. Tricia had and has a strong ethical code and sense of personal responsibility. In fact, she is one of the most honorable human beings I know.

I am not suggesting this strategy of firmly holding the line for everyone. Tricia had/has a unique level of mathematical, networking, and communication skills, and a particular value in this type of organization. She had a very strong position from which to negotiate. Had they not backed down, Tricia would have followed through with her low self-rating because, for her, it was the *right* thing to do. Again, I'm very aware of the concessions we all must make in life. Tricia's decision in this case, though not translatable to everyone's circumstances, provides one of the strongest real-life examples of the principles of responsibility and accountability that are at the heart of this book.

Tricia is now a high level executive in a global corporation, and it is not surprising that among her greatest strengths are that her employees, direct reports, administrators, and CEOs are aware of her personal and professional code of responsibility and ethics. My friends tell me I hit the lottery when I met Tricia. I agree!

> **TO CONSIDER:** When has "Talk the Talk" and "Walk the Walk" become one?

Be Honest

I have included examples of some of the most powerful people in the world being unwilling to be honest, and what it might look and sound like if they were. Here is an example about our oldest daughter, Samantha, when it was entirely possible that being honest would cost her a job:

She was a student at the Institute of Technology for Computer Engineering, and one component of the program included a several months-long internship. Samantha was really intrigued by a certain NASA program, but had virtually no experience in aeronautics or that specific field of Computer Networking. (My daughter tells me there are significant differences between Computer Engineering and Computer Networking, and I take her word for it!) Sammy talked to her mom and me, and we encouraged her to go for it if it was what interested her. Sam was still quite nervous about not having specific experience in any type of aeronautics. Tricia and I suggested she do some serious reading about NASA, and during the interview be completely honest and candid about what she knows, and what she does not know. We also added, be honest with yourself; if accepted, are you ready to do the work required? If the answer is yes, let the interviewer know you will work incredibly hard to learn whatever is required and/or helpful. My wife and I belabored the point that Sammy would have to be fully committed if chosen.

Sammy applied and got a phone interview, during which she was questioned about several types of programming languages, some of which she was not familiar with, and Sammy fully acknowledged what she did and did not know. She also told the interviewer if accepted she would work "super hard." Later, Samantha received an email congratulating and accepting her as a part of the NASA team for a 4 month paid internship in Cape Canaveral, Florida! The person who originally interviewed Sammy, Kelvin Ruiz, was also her supervisor during her internship, and became a wonderful and gracious mentor for Samantha as well. At the end of her tenure, it was discreetly communicated that a significant reason she was accepted into the NASA program was her very strong mathematics and Computer Engineering background, and they were also impressed that she said out loud she didn't have any experience in Computer Networking.

Samantha's honesty and transparency showed them she was someone who would be teachable, and they were thrilled to teach her whatever she could absorb during her internship. Mr. Ruiz's willingness to share his knowledge and experience openly, straightforwardly, and passionately is the mark of a true mentor. This is a beautiful example of Internal Accountability and responsibility for both mentor and student!

Samantha finished her summer internship, she had the opportunity to work on the future mission to Mars, and was offered another internship at NASA, which is the path for a full-time position. When Samantha gave me a tour of NASA, I thought I might pop with pride!

> **TO CONSIDER:** When did being honest feel great? (Full disclosure: I'm still not completely clear on the difference between Computer Networking and Computer Engineering!)

Are We Monsters?

MONSTERS INC. is an animated film by Disney/Pixar. Pixar is known for films that breathe life into the computer animated characters, are grounded by a compelling story (often a universal truth), and have a cast of skilled actors who lend their vocal talents to embodying colorful creatures. *MONSTERS INC.* is the story of monsters Mike Wazowski (voiced by Billy Crystal) and James P. "Sully" Sullivan (voiced by John Goodman), who are gainfully employed in a factory called Monsters Inc. where they, along with other employees, are able to transport from their world into our world and scare children out of their minds. We learn that this corporation does this to "capture" the screams and terror of the children to provide power to their world. In fact, their mantra is "we scare because we care." Paradoxically these "Monsters" are actually afraid of children, and one child ("Boo") follows a monster through the portal from our world into the world of Monsters Inc. Eventually Boo and Sully begin to see each other not as terrifying creatures, but as beings who care for each other. In one beautiful scene, Sulley proudly shows Boo a film of him transporting to the dark closest of a little boy, terrifyingly emerging, and subsequently scaring the living heck out of the youngster. Sulley has a great deal of pride in his ability to do his job, and his face has an expression of thrilled excitement. At one point Sully looks at Boo and realizes she is cowering, distraught, and scared, rather than sharing in the feelings of pride and excitement. In an incredible display of the possibilities of creativity, skill, and computer animation—this new generation of animators are able to articulate millions of individual hairs—Sulley's face transforms from joy to despair as he is struck with the awful realization of the harm he and the other monsters have been inflicting on millions of children, just like his little friend Boo.

I think it is a beautiful example of a universal truth. We might think we are doing something good until we see it in a different context. Like Dr. Rina Dubin said, the context makes a difference. Sometimes I describe it as, doing the right thing in the wrong way. When adults say things like, "I'm a great partner / father / mother / wife / husband / person, etc.," I sometimes share the Monsters Inc. story. I believe we all have times on the screen like Sully showed Boo. That's what makes us human (and occasionally monsters ourselves).

> **TO CONSIDER:** When has something presented in a humorous way resonated with you?

Pay It Forward

Miley Cyrus

At an early point in Miley Cyrus' career (as an actor and singer), she starred in a very popular TV show named *Hannah Montana*. Hannah Montana was a series about a young girl, who led a regular life by day, but unbeknownst to the public, was Hannah Montana—a young singer superstar. Our youngest daughter, Christina, watched the show faithfully, and when she heard Miley Cyrus was going to appear in Rhode Island as the Hannah Montana character, she just about vibrated out of her skin when her mother and I told her we had already bought tickets. We went to the show, and Miley Cyrus appeared as her TV character, blond wig and all, for the first set. Even at such a young age, once she began the concert it was apparent she was already a seasoned pro. Ms. Cyrus was even more impressive when she appeared for the second set, as herself. During her last song, on stage, alone with just an acoustic guitar, it was clear she had the special stuff. But *here's* the thing.

The day she was performing, she and her father, Billy Ray Cyrus, made a trip to the Hasbro Children's Hospital. Most of the children hospitalized there were (and are) facing great adversity, and some would never see another year. Ms. Cyrus and her dad went there, no fanfare, no cameras, no television crew, no news reporters, and spent time with those kids. A few days after the concert there was just a tiny blurb in the local paper. I can personally guarantee you those children had an incredible time; a truly special moment in their lives. What an example of paying it forward! There are many beautiful examples of famous people in the world like: Michelle Obama; Oprah Winfrey; Malala Yousafzai; George Clooney, Brad Pitt, and Matt Damon; Viola Davis; Mariska Hargitay; Stefani J. A. Germanotta; and Taylor Swift; or your favorite, actor, singer or sports star, paying it forward. But being famous is not a requirement. Whether you are well-known or not, paying it forward, in any capacity, is a unique and special gift, to *both* the receiver and the giver.

Al Colella

As a family, we have had a long history with volunteering. The girls, now young women, have been significantly influenced by their grandfather in this regard. Al Colella, Tricia's Dad, started a movement in which people from a local church in Rhode Island began to support St. Ann's parish in the South Bronx of New York. Over the years, we have taken many trips to St. Ann's. There we would do whatever would be helpful for the children and families such as: repairing the physical structure and grounds, securing funds for a major renovation, establishing a library, and providing multiple computers to create a learning center. We have had extraordinary experiences there, and I would like to share one.

During these trips, when Al was walking around the grounds of St. Ann's, it was like watching the Pied Piper. A dozen or so children of multiple backgrounds would often be following him just about everywhere he went. Now to add some context, Al is an eighty-year-old, Italian, bald, white (really white!), former football player, hazel/blue eyed man.

Al is a person who acknowledges the very real fact that the old cliche of "I don't see color" is actually a form of subtle racism in itself, since by saying you don't see color, you are not acknowledging the reality, for minorities, the color of their skin DOES have an impact on their lives; because we live in a society where systemic racism has been woven in since the beginning. He is acutely aware of the oppression of race in our country, especially regarding the bias in education, and has written two books on the subject.

I believe Al is an example of how people, especially children, know when someone sees their intrinsic value. This subject can be multi-layered with discussions of cultural bias and something called implicit bias, which is a bias so ingrained we don't even know it's there. I stand before you guilty of both. But, I believe the ability to treat someone with dignity, respect, kindness, and compassion, is something that resonates with children regardless of their socioeconomic situation, ethnicity, or color, in a very profound and heartfelt way. I believe these traits are woven into the very fabric of paying it forward.

> **TO CONSIDER:** In what ways do you, or want, to pay it forward?

Youth is Not Wasted on the Young— the Inability to Truly Listen

Our youngest daughter, Christina, has taught me some very valuable lessons. At the time of this writing Christina (Paco) was 19 years old. We have had many talks about equal rights, principles, oppression, etc. About two years ago, she was talking about the Black Lives Matter movement. I listened to her impassioned conceptualization of the movement and when she was finished, I responded, really countered, with, "Well, Christina, everyone's lives matter regardless of the color of their skin." I also said this in a way inferred I saw the big picture and she *really* didn't know what the heck she was talking about.

Fast forward two years to March of 2020 and Christina and I were still having that debate. Yes, that's right, *two years*. It was a contentious sticking point for us and a source of potential conflict. But this time was different. I'm confident there was a confluence of influences including the horrible things happening to black Americans during this time. You might be saying to yourself, "David, what the ####, they have been happening all along," and you would be right. I'm embarrassed, really feel Shame, to say that somehow the plight of racism alone was not enough for me to question why I kept saying, or least thinking "All Lives Matter" when we would talk about BLACK LIVES MATTER. Something Ann Sinko had said in her interview (see Appendix B) regarding my grandparents' immigration to the United States—"at least they had a suitcase"—*felt* different. That statement had some glue on it. However, for this latest conversation with Paco, *I* did something different.

Instead of me locking into the same unproductive framework, I took some time *before* we talked and asked my parts to give me some space during this conversation (they consented), asked my parts to trust Self and Self-energy when discussing this with Christina (they were willing), and asked the entire system to be conscious of the 8 C's, and especially asked my system to remain *curious* about the topic and her viewpoint. During that last conversation (lucky for me), one drop of water found the seed, and the perspective of Black Lives Matter broke through the encapsulated shell that was my protective system. Of course all human beings' lives are valuable, but I was missing the point. I will never understand experientially what it's like to live as a black person in this country, but I believe I now have a better understanding of the Black Lives Matter slogan and movement. The way our country and culture developed, Black Lives (didn't/don't) Matter (or not nearly as much). Legacy burdens, revisionist history, white privilege, Cognitive Physio Mechanisms were/are all woven into my protective shield. What I really missed in the conversations with Christina, and the profound message of Black Lives Matter, is the contextual framework. I now realize when I would say "everyone's lives matter" in the context of the Black Lives Matter movement it diminishes, undermines, and invalidates their history and the message. In addition, when I would say this to Christina in the context of these conversations, it was akin to a red herring. Instead of addressing the painful reality, I changed the context of the discussion, ignored the message, and missed the point entirely. Thank you Christina, and thank you my friends. I am sorry it took me so long to even get to this point. I've got work to do.

> **TO CONSIDER:** My mind is kind of blown. I'm going to spend time with my system.

CHAPTER 12

LOFTY GOALS

As we have seen, there can be many paths to embrace the universal truths we aspire to, and there are specific requirements to undertake such an endeavor.

Lofty goals require a solid underpinning that can withstand the pressures and stresses of the structure it must support.

This book's underpinnings and foundation are the universal truths which are self-evident and we hold dear. The framework resting on this foundation consists of five stages: 1) Identifying a problem exists (i.e. the diminishment of civility in our society) 2) Fueling the hope we can make it better, 3) Developing a consensus on *what* are the specific goals we will achieve, and 4) Thoughtfully and courageously asking ourselves, even if it's painful, why are we languishing in our quest? Then we can collectively move to 5) *How* we can achieve these goals and be in the leadership role of our own change/growth/movement towards responsibility and civility. But we have to reach a critical mass of individuals in the population to carry our culture forward to where we should be. More than that, we have to take collective action to select our leaders well, and ensure that they are the people we truly want not only to represent us, but to influence and set the tone for the society we live in—with the goal of being part of a civil society.

It's become a cliche to say that our country has never been more divided. With the exception of Abraham Lincoln's presidency during the Civil War, it's absolutely true. And the worst part of it is that the divisions are being pushed by those at the top. Partisanship, rather than leadership, has come to dominate. We need to remember what good leadership looks like.

Being a responsible public servant in a position of leadership and power does not quite have the same end goal as being the CEO of a company, but I do believe that we can learn a lot from the business world about what makes a good leader. (Though it is certainly not lost on me that our current President, who was supposed to be such a successful entrepreneur, ran for office touting that his alleged business acumen would allow him to do great things for the country. We all know what a mess his companies are.)

Good to Great, by Jim Collins, is a fascinating exploration of corporate America, a cautionary tale, and an encouraging path for hope and success even outside the context of business. Collins and his team did an exhaustive amount of research on companies at critical moments of change. Some companies that had experienced long periods of success were unable to survive these periods of transition. Conversely, thanks to proper leadership and vision, a relatively small number of companies were able to not just survive, but adapt at these critical junctures, and transition from a good company to a great company. The extensive research team of *Good to Great* came to the conclusion that regardless of the type of company, or if the business or economy was stable or not, all companies that transitioned from good to great had what they called "Level 5 leaders."

Chapter 2 of *Good to Great* is dedicated entirely to empirically-derived observations and conclusions about the qualities of these exemplary CEOs.

"Level 5 leaders look out the window to attribute success to factors other than themselves. When things go poorly, however, they look in the mirror and blame themselves, taking full responsibility" (p 39). Collins states that it is not that Level 5 leaders have no sense of ego, ambition, initiative, or drive. In fact, to be this kind of leader, you must have a strong sense of self and possess those qualities, but the goal of building something great with an enduring structure and legacy has to be more important than your personal accolades. In fact, modesty—yes, *modesty*—has been cited as a consistent characteristic in Level 5 leaders!

Lofty Goals

Collins calls out the mistaken belief that good leaders are ones with high visibility, who toot their own horn, tell it like it is, and tout themselves as a person who will single-handedly guide us to prosperity. In fact, the CEOs that embodied some, most, or all of the above-referenced qualities did not fare very well. Let me revise that. The CEO's probably fared *very* well—for themselves. However, the company and employees did not. (We've all heard of the term "golden parachute.")

Responsibility, humility, honesty, giving credit to others, and acknowledging the impact of luck, are all qualities of Level 5 leaders. When we elect leaders who do not embody these characteristics—even if there is a short term gain (which could last for years)—the longer term prospects are not good. Astutely, Collins notes that while Level 5 leaders consistently established a foundation and framework to continue to build a successful enterprise—especially after their tenure, in example after example—egocentric-driven leadership resulted in a company being mired in mediocrity, or the crippling of a company over time.

Diametrically opposed to a Level 5 leader's legacy of continued success, especially after their departure, egocentric leaders leave a different type of legacy—more like what IFS would refer to as a legacy burden. But this would never register as an indictment with these lesser leaders. If a company fails after the departure of a CEO who is ego-centric, "what better testament to your own personal greatness that the place falls apart after you leave" (p. 26).

A cautionary tale indeed!

Good to Great explores some universal truths. True leaders, in my interpretation of what Collins defines as Level 5 Leaders, embody characteristics such as being humble, civil (and not the most rudimentary definition of the word), courageous, creative, confident, responsible, and accountable. And the institutions they build could be said to be Self-led. Collins identifies enduring organizations with Level 5 leaders who built an *internal* "culture of discipline" and places them in stark comparison to the lesser leaders—whose concept of discipline was dominance, force, or punishment. (p. 124).

Now, think about when President Trump tweeted, after the protests against police brutality, that we had to "dominate" protestors, and "When the looting starts, the shooting starts." What sort of a leader was that?

It may be futile to argue the point, but I am actually *not* anti-Trump. My concern is that those who lead set an example. Every section of society can more fully embrace civility, responsibility, and Internal and External Accountability with strong, great leadership. While all of us aren't Level 5 leaders, we all have the right to choose who will be elected to represent us. I have absolute confidence we can individually and collectively set a foundation different from the one that has been established over the last few years. In this context, Dr. Milgram's experiments and conclusions about the influence and impact of authority figures feel especially poignant, and ominous.

New Perspectives

With different leadership at the helm, could we find a way to embrace, as a culture and country, civility as a reasonable and desirable characteristic of being a human being? While we might need to start with the most rudimentary definition—"merely refraining from rudeness, being polite in a perfunctory way"—that will not result in a *civil* society. I respectfully suggest that we individually, and as a country, reach higher. What would it be like to stand together as representatives of whatever country, culture, religion, or political party we belong to and still be part of a civil society? Could we create a movement to be, at the very least civil, and aim for civility, dignity and respect?

To do this, we would need to make a decision to be responsible and make a commitment to follow this path. It starts with an individual commitment. Will everyone be civil? Of course not! But we could join together to create a critical mass of civility in our country. A Force—that would be something!

Could we embrace differences of opinion—as a *culture and country*— and when we disagree, do so as reasonable people? Could we embrace differences of what is God, a higher power, or however you embrace a higher power (or don't, for that matter)? Could political parties embrace the concept of non-partisan motivated decisions concerning what would

Lofty Goals

be best for all, instead of what party sponsored the bill or legislation? Could we vote for representatives of our city, state, and federal government who lead by example and who would vote on the merits of the bill, not their party affiliation? I know this is an antiquated term from my band days, but could we make it *cool* to be civil?

Could we embrace our creativity and the ability to imagine, as a *culture, country, and beyond*, like the John Lennon song? Imagine if all the religions in the world decided to *fully* embrace the Universal Truth: "Do unto others, as you would have them do unto you." Imagine if the focus, energy, and influence of religious institutions was not our "God is the right God, our religion is the right religion, or our Messiah is the right Messiah." Imagine integrating religious hierarchies with all people, not based upon gender (or any expression of gender), or sexual orientation. Imagine if women throughout the world could say, "I will support my religious institution when we are represented in the hierarchy by having the opportunity of becoming Bishops, Cardinals, and the Pope." I bet you it would not take long for religious institutions to revisit their positions and to eventually acknowledge that the concept of justification has played a significant role *in relegating half of the world's population to second-class status.* Let me revise that; it could take a *very* long time, but it could be done.

It would start inside us, like in Internal Family Systems, or whatever model or template works for you. It would start with how we treat our people regardless of shade, color, culture, religion, or economic status. It would mean that we look to be "good enough" with everyone: children, wives, husbands, partners, families—and outward through our communities. It would mean, inevitably, that we would have to work on righting wrongs on individual and collective levels.

So, before we conclude, I would like to revisit two of the original definitions I used in Chapter 1, and augment them to reflect the experience, knowledge, and wisdom of the many people who have influenced this book. I respectfully offer these new definitions together as a goal for all of us, as a culture and country.

DAVID MEDEIROS

The Principle of Responsibility & Civility Redefined

The Principle of Responsibility: The ability to respond and act in accordance with universal truths grounded in morality, such as "Do unto others as you would have them do unto you," the Principle of Dignity and Respect, and to recognize the intrinsic value of all human beings. To be able to more fully embody the entity and qualities of Self—however you may define it—with qualities such as compassion, civility, dignity, respect, and kindness, and to guide us to be curious and compassionate towards ourselves and others when we are not. Furthermore, responsibility includes a framework—a type of duty to acknowledge, to attend, and to ameliorate the pain and suffering of oppressed people, groups, and cultures.

Civility: That which occurs when people treat each other with dignity, respect, and kindness, and embrace the interconnectedness and inherent value of all human beings and the planet we live on.

CONCLUSION

My story begins and ends with drums. I have always been drawn to the pulse and beat of music. During an Internal Family Systems training I was a part of, I became friends with two incredibly skilled clinicians: Meghan Gehman and David Keevil—who are talented musicians as well. Meg is a guitar player, fantastic vocalist, and writes great songs. David, known internationally as David K., plays bass guitar and a ***mean*** harmonica. We talked about playing together and eventually set a date. I had an opportunity to play drums thirty-five years after my last gig! I brought my drums out of storage, began to practice a bit, and eventually played a gig with Meg and David. Guess what? The same problems I experienced thrity-five to forty years ago were evident again. My sense of time and tempo was not solid, and as the show went on I became more and more frustrated and tense. The more frustrated and tense I became the more and more my time wavered. It was not fun for me at all. I had not experienced something like this in decades. I drove home that night in a foul mood. Well, I was ready to not play drums anymore, and later I called Meg and told her. Meg listened and then she just said this little thing, "I wouldn't be ready to give up on it so soon."

I thought, "SO soon, really? SO soon, after all these years. REALLY MEG?! You have no idea." What I said was, "Well, this has been a problem for a long time."

LATER, a little light flickered, or more accurately—a seed. Not just any seed! This seed was like one that had remained dormant, in an incredibly inhospitable desert environment, for many years. Somehow its capacity for life is not extinguished by harsh temperatures, brutal conditions, lack of water, etc. But eventually rain does come, at the right time of year, with the right kind of temperatures, right level of sunlight, and the seed germinates and blooms. This is what happened to the seed that was planted so many years ago at the Casino by the Sea with Kenny Jo.

I began to think about what I have learned about responsibility and accountability since that conversation, and Kenny's recommendation of taking lessons with Gary Chaffee. I did an internet search for Mr. Chaffee and saw he was giving lessons via Skype. I reached out numerous times, but all my attempts were initially unsuccessful. I kept trying, and this was the last sequence of emails.

From: David Medeiros <davidmedeirostherapy@gmail.com>
Date: Jun 25, 2019 at 8:10 PM EDT
To: Gary Chaffee <   >

Hi Mr. Chaffee. I am looking to confirm this is your email address since there are people who claim to be you on Facebook.

I want to schedule Skype lessons primarily focused on time keeping. I have struggled in this area for a long time. It was Kenny Jo Silva from Beaver Brown who recommended you many years ago when I was playing and recording with Steve Smith and the Nakeds. Not Steve Smith the drummer.

Best,
David Medeiros

From: Gary Chaffee <   >
Date: Jun 26, 2019 at 1:36 PM EDT
To: David Medeiros <davidmedeirostherapy@gmail.com>

I'm no longer teaching here or on Skype.

Gary

Conclusion

From: David Medeiros <davidmedeirostherapy@gmail.com>
Date: Jun 26, 2019 at 2:40 PM EDT
To: Gary Chaffee <   >

Thanks for responding, Mr. Chaffee. Are you teaching in any capacity or in a clinic situation?

Best,
David Medeiros

From: David Medeiros <davidmedeirostherapy@gmail.com>
Date: June 26, 2019 at 6:17:33 PM EDT
To: Gary Chaffee <   >
Subject: Re: response

Mr. Chaffee.

Also, a little background: As I mentioned Kenny Jo Silva from John Cafferty and Beaver Brown recommended you about 40 years ago when they were recording the Eddie and the Cruisers soundtrack. I was getting ready to record as well. Kenny knew I struggled with keeping time and strongly suggested he could provide an introduction and shared the improvement he had experienced while working with you. I was not in a place to "hear" him and insisted I would figure it out on my own. I never did. I am now a psychotherapist and present/teach nationally and use this story to illustrate how "parts" of us can prevent a person from being open for help.

Since that time, I have traveled throughout the country to work with the best teachers I can find and have the privilege to teach others now.

I brought my drums out of storage about 5 months ago and played my first gig last week. I'm confident you can guess, I struggled with my time keeping.

If you would be willing to have a lesson, or a few, (in any form) with me it would be greatly appreciated. And, if it is not right for you, I still want to thank you for all you have done as a player and true teacher. Lastly, I want to let you know you, and your teaching acumen, were a part of one of my greatest life lessons.

All my best,
David

From: Gary Chaffee <   >
Date: June 27, 2019 at 3:11:02 PM EDT
To: David Medeiros <davidmedeirostherapy@gmail.com>
Subject: Re: response

David,

You are very persistent! Okay, although I am completely retired and have cancelled all of my students I'll agree to give you 1 lesson where we will see if I can help you with your issues.

I only do 2-hour lessons and the rate is $( ). Don't know if you're talking about an in-person lesson or Skype. (I assume the former.) We would need to find a time and since my wife and I are planning on spending a lot more time at our house in VT we would need to get that squared away sooner rather than later. We are leaving this Friday and will be back after the holiday

Maybe Tuesday the 9th around noon. Let me know.

Gary

Several emails later we set up a day and time for my lesson.

I went to the lesson, and while Mr. Chaffee was gracious he was clear this would be a "one and done" lesson. After 2.5 hours he said, "You're an interesting fellow, like an unpainted canvas. I'll teach you." On the outside

Conclusion

I was cool and collected (or maybe I thought I was!). Inside I felt like jumping up and down! I have taken lessons from Mr. Chaffee for over a year, and it is a rare privilege to sit with him. He is both a Master Teacher and Master Player. My time-feel has continued to improve, is better than ever actually, and I get the rare chance at a "do over" 40 years later. My life would have been complete had I not been able to do this with Mr. Chaffee, but to do something I love with joy and growing confidence is a special gift. However, the biggest gift was planting the seed for a life lesson about responsibility, bringing clarity to the concept of Internal and External Accountability, learning how our *parts* are well intended, and embracing the conviction that Self and Self-Energy are a powerful force.

May the force be with you!

Gary Chaffee and me

For quite some time I have thought this last story would serve as the end of this book. Given where we *all* are in such a transitional period in our country, and the gravity of what's at stake, I can no longer do so. The challenges we face concerning how we embrace the universal truths such as the Principles of Dignity and Respect, "Do unto others", responsibility, accountability, and civility are being severely tested. Many of the current challenges and injustices we face have existed since the conception of our constitution. In the year 2020, we are experiencing a level of divisiveness and polarization that arguably has not been so clearly visible since the Civil War. Perhaps the internet, social media, video phones, etc. have had a positive influence at this time in our history in that we have more information about what our leaders stand for, and they are not as shrouded in mystery. Our history is replete with examples of what happens when people and countries are at the tumultuous transition points and there is a systemic and institutionalized justification of *Us* against *Them*. Elie Wizel and so many others are absolutely clear about what happens when we turn away. We have an opportunity to vote for who represents us. Millions and millions of human beings have given their lives "just" to have that opportunity.

Let's not turn away, but turn towards. Let's turn toward an inclusive, rather than an exclusive model, of how we interpret and practice universal truths, and have compassion for ourselves and others when we struggle. Let's, as a people, renew our collective commitment that we are *all deserving* of being treated with dignity and respect, and that the idiom: "Do unto others as you would have them do unto you", would be practiced without conditions of color, race, gender, or religion. Let's turn towards continuing to have the courage to look inward—even at the darkest places—and to work to be individually and collectively responsible and accountable. Our paths may be different, but our destination would be the same, to be and live in a truly civil society. Will it be hard to accomplish this? Of course! But we can do it. The opportunity is ours. It's time. It's time for a call to action.

With respect, David Medeiros

APPENDIX A

Cognitive Physio Mechanisms (CPM)

I have been influenced by: Aaron T. Beck who is considered the father of Cognitive Behavioral Therapy, and Anna Freud and her landmark book *The Ego and its Mechanisms of Defense*, and theorists such as Bessel van der Kolk concerning the integration, impact, and importance of physiology in psychology—especially trauma.

Conceptually, I believe the cognitive aspect of a CPM is the thinking process of parts (in IFS language), and the mechanism is how our parts shield and protect our internal system—with an emphasis on how this information is processed not only in our minds, but just as importantly how it is encoded and experienced in our bodies.

Cognitive Behavioral Therapy, as delineated by its name, is primarily focused on the processing of the prefrontal cortex—the thinking part of our brains. As Bessel van der Kolk has articulated, it's our limbic system and our entire body which keeps the score of where intense, traumatic memories are stored. Thus, I have concerns about utilizing CBT in trauma work. For example, I treat many adult victims of childhood sexual abuse. Even though the adult that sits in front of me (often) intellectually understands it was not their fault, I cannot remember many times in my career when a client, during the process of healing, has not said, "I know I didn't do something wrong, but I can't help thinking I *did do* something wrong, I can still sense it, this part of my body hurts when I talk about this, I didn't fight back, I fought back too much, it haunts me, I had an orgasm, I was provocative, I'm damaged, I'm dirty," etc. In addition, it is quite common for victims of sexual abuse to experience visceral and physiological distress when thinking about abuse that happened decades ago. Furthermore, utilizing Cognitive Behavioral Therapy in trauma work may inadvertently lead a person to believe they are not trying hard enough, i.e. "I know blaming myself is a cognitive distortion and yet I still feel I did something wrong, I can't get it out of my head, I was responsible in some way, I must try harder, it's hopeless," or "I will never be free of this." CBT does have methods for desensitizing the intensity of traumatically-encoded memories, but not the critical *reprocessing* component. I am not suggesting this is a conscious effort by well-meaning CBT specialists, however, we know trauma is not stored in our prefrontal cortex (located in our frontal lobe) but in our reptilian brains (our limbic system), and our bodies. Modalities such as IFS, EMDR, neurofeedback, somatically grounded therapies, yoga, dance, and performance art, can address, *reprocess,* and heal these deeply-encoded memories.

Here are the remaining 3 Cognitive Physio Mechanisms (CPMs) that are often evident when there is erosion of universal truths. With all the CPMs, there is a physiological component of how we internalize the incoming information, which usually leads to take, or not. The paradox, as we know in the practice of Tai Chi, *not* taking action, *is* an action in-and-of-itself.

Dr. Francis Pescosolido's office

Denial is a CPM whereby we shield and protect ourselves from unwanted thoughts, feelings, behaviors, and consequences by simply not acknowledging the existence, impact, or causality of them.

Minimization is a CPM whereby we shield and protect ourselves from unwanted thoughts, feelings, behaviors, or consequences by simply making the experience smaller and smaller until the importance and/or impact is diminished or even dismissed. The smaller something becomes, the less important it becomes.

Dichotomy is a CPM whereby we shield or protect ourselves from unwanted thoughts, feelings, behaviors, or consequences by reducing the world to a black- and-white, either-or, or on-off template. The use of this mechanism is seductive in that it reduces our internal and external experiences to a rigid framework, and therefore we experience life in absolutes, regardless of the contextual framework. This mechanism can also bypass the effort and process of addressing complicated situations by offering seemingly straightforward but inaccurate solutions. For instance, that building a wall will address the very complicated and multi-layered issue of illegal immigration in the United States. If: "No wall = there are problems" and we don't want "problems", so, all we have to do is build a wall—problem solved! It's that easy!

Explaining CPM to Kids

I work with children and have come up with a way to demonstrate the CPM concept in a way they can understand, and have some fun while we are doing it. I have an old fashioned meat grinder in my office. I use it to show that no matter what we put in it, if we turn the hand crank, it's going to come out in the shape of the disk at the bottom of the grinder. If the disk has many small holes, whatever we put in the top of the grinder will come out looking like the hamburger meat you buy in a supermarket. In my clinical practice with children, we put play dough or clay in the top opening, turn the handle to grind it, and look as it comes out of the metal disk. It *always* comes out in the shape of hamburger meat you buy in the grocery store. After a short, age-appropriate discussion on CPM we may try changing the disk on the grinder, from the one that makes the noodle-like shape of hamburger meat, to a disk which has a different shape. I use a disk which has a triangle shape, like you might see in those play dough kits. For my second example we put the same material into the top of the grinder, we turn the handle (I usually add a "PRESTO!" for drama), and it comes out in the shape of a triangle. No matter how many times we put the stuff in the grinder it will come out in the shape of the new disk. Every single time. Instead of telling kids they need to switch the disks/their thinking, now we can begin to explore *why* they may.

APPENDIX B

Interviews with Ann Sinko, LMFT; Rina Dubin, Ed.D.; and Michael Elkin, LMFT

Ann Sinko, LMFT

Ann Sinko is a Master Teacher and therapist. In addition to putting in the proverbial ten thousand hours of study and practice towards IFS, she has some very unique gifts. I would consider her an empath for her ability to connect and show compassion for others. Ann has had many teachers and mentors, and has a seemingly unquenchable thirst for knowledge and exploration. Her expertise with IFS and legacy burdens within an IFS framework makes her an important participant, as I personally believe the healing which needs to take place in our country has its roots in this concept and process. Ann has often shared with her students that she learned this technique/ability to conceptualize and work with legacy burdens from one of her mentors, Michi Rose, Ph.D.—a biologist who later became a therapist, and also trained in Shamanism.

DAVID: I'd like to talk to you about the constructs of responsibility and accountability, and also integrate them along with how legacy burdens impact these concepts as well.

ANN: And I sent you an article on white supremacy culture.

DAVID: (pause) I don't recall seeing it.

ANN: So I'm going to send it. I just sent it now.

DAVID: If I said, *Oh I've read it, and it was so helpful; thank you so much, Ann,* it would kind of defeat the purpose of this book.

ANN & DAVID: (We both laugh.)

DAVID: Oh, I just pulled it up, I'll read it. (*White Supremacy Culture,* by Tema Okun. dRworks)

ANN: At the IFS trainer retreat, we had this lovely young woman come in [Sydnee R. Corriders, LMSW] and do a day of diversity for us. She had us read this article and it lists white supremacy culture. So again, making it systemic, institutionalized systemic, instead of a white supremacist. And she talked about how we all adhere to these because it's what's valued in our society. Then it talks [the article] about the antidote to them. So, I just have found it so helpful. I thought it would be helpful in your writing process.

DAVID: Yes. When we're done, I'll read it. Thank you. So, for the readers, and hopefully there's readers, could you briefly define what a legacy burden is?

ANN: Yes. So, legacy burdens are behaviors, thoughts, feelings, and energies that get passed down through generational lines or through culture. And they can be directly or indirectly passed down. Energetic ones could be passed down in a more indirect way. Just listening to what our families value, their beliefs, and the way they teach us, is a way to transmit energetic legacy burdens.

DAVID: All right, an indirect way might be like a feeling or expression passed down energetically, rather than something which was verbalized, but it is still there. For instance, [the inference] you shouldn't talk about a particular race in a positive way, even though it might not be actually stated.

Appendix B: Interviews with Ann Sinko, Rina Dubin & Michael Elkin

ANN: Yes. So, on this day of diversity training, she addressed that. Very quickly she asked, *So what were your first learnings about black people, or your first learnings about white people? What were your first learnings about Hispanic people? What were your first learnings about Asian people?* It was fascinating.

DAVID: So, an energetic legacy burden might be passed down through generations implicitly?

ANN: Yes, the meaning, intent, and content of an energetic legacy burden can still be passed down, but the origin can remain unknown.

ANN: Our implicit biases come from legacy burdens and cultural burdens. They're a belief that we took on from growing up in the family and culture that we did.

DAVID: At the end of every chapter, I have a little section, "To consider." In this section, I ask the reader to ponder questions, several of which are related to legacy and cultural burdens such as: *Where did you learn your concept of: responsibility, civility, your moral compass? When did you learn it? How has it impacted your beliefs?*

ANN: Yes, the leader of the diversity training addressed those questions. It was fascinating to bring awareness to my first memories of biases.

DAVID: From your personal perspective, how would you define responsibility?

ANN: Well, the first thing that came into my head was Michael's [Mike Elkin's] definition, which is "the ability to respond". Okay, and I don't think that's complete enough. So, there are two areas that came into my head: responsible to and responsible for. And they're different. We're responsible for our children until they get to a certain age. But we're responsible to our spouses, not for our spouses. I see that as really different.

I guess I see responsibility is acting respectfully. I suppose duty in a way that's congruent with our values, but that doesn't really work because you could have really bad values. I don't want to bring in the word *morally* but it kind of belongs, yes?

DAVID: Yes, Yes. There's a real slippery slope to define something like this, and then to have a level of moral judgment in it. But I do believe the word *morals* or something akin to that word, is the foundation of the base definition I use for responsibility. Responsibility is to know for oneself between right and wrong.

ANN: That's morality, isn't it?

DAVID: Yes. Oftentimes, a discussion of morality can seem very black-and-white, and morally judgmental. I don't personally think of it [responsibility] like that. Because like you said, it's not only a black-and white-thing. However, it's hard to imagine the Nazi parties regime wasn't black-and-white. So, it [right and wrong] can be black-and-white for those kinds of scenarios. But there are a lot of different aspects in this exploration, especially through the lens of IFS, where parts have positive intent.

ANN: Yes, and I guess in terms of our roles, we have role responsibility. And then there's overarching human responsibilities.

DAVID: Okay, so, when you would think of responsibility from an IFS perspective, would it be the same?

ANN: It would. I think that's why I'm so taken with IFS, because it fits with my beliefs and values. I didn't have to adopt anything. And I think that's my worldview and the way I think. I don't think I can separate me from IFS anymore.

DAVID: So what are your thoughts about some people that really seem to abdicate their sense of responsibility?

ANN: I think that it's about fear. It's about the burdens peoples' parts take on. And I think it's about adhering to the Rules of Shame. And, the rules of Shame are what our Managers parts do to try to keep us away from shame and our vulnerabilities. Manager parts adhere to the rules of perfectionism and control. They abide to the ways that they think they should be, and they think they're acting responsibly by not rocking the boat, but they're not at all. It's all fear driven.

DAVID: From your personal perspective, how would you define civility?

ANN: Civility is just seeing that we are all connected and that we deserve to be treated with respect and kindness. That, if you hurt one person, you are really hurting everybody.

DAVID: And would that [definition] dovetail with IFS as well? The IFS lens of civility?

ANN: Well, when we're in Self, we know that we're all connected. And, we're going to treat people from a place of kindness, compassion, clarity, and curiosity. When our parts get in the way, they lose perspective and don't act with civility.

DAVID: Thank you. Do you feel a standard of responsibility and civility has eroded over time in our country in our world, and what would you attribute this to?

ANN: Absolutely. Again, I think it's about fear. It's about scarcity, unchallenged beliefs, and our legacy burdens. You know the: *not enough, not enough for me, I've got to get mine,* mentality. It's individualism, consumerism, materialism, perfectionism—"isms" are all institutionalized ways of being that are eroding civility and responsibility.

DAVID: Do you believe that's especially poignant now? In the current administration?

ANN: Absolutely. Absolutely. You know, I've been so sorely disappointed in leadership on so many levels during this COVID thing. When you have good leadership, it makes all the difference. It's a pandemic. So what are they going to do? You know they can't make it go away, but they can show up, and if they're in Self, and a position of power, their message can really help calm people down, and you can speak to them in a way that helps them cope with what's going on. There's been a severe lack of that, I think on so many levels, so many levels.

DAVID: Like when President Trump said that the CDC had suggested that everyone wear masks, and yet in the same press conference, he said, *but I'm not probably going to do that.* That alone to me was very poignant. It spoke volumes. It polarized.

ANN: Instead of people coming together, it polarized. It really did a disservice to the nation. We all need role models.

DAVID: People like Nelson Mandela, Martin Luther King, and Susan B. Anthony, rather than polarize, actually unify under the most harsh, often horrific, circumstances.

ANN: Yes. That's what good leadership does.

DAVID: So, I think that answers the next question which is: *Do you believe leaders have an impact on how citizens embrace or reject responsibility and civility?*

ANN: Yes. So, that's right, they either have the ability to harmonize or polarize, and everything in between.

DAVID: This is always an interesting question for me. Do you believe in the innate good in people, and if so, how do you grapple with the fact that human beings—usually men—in almost all cultures, countries, and throughout recorded history, continue to oppress and subjugate?

ANN: Well, in some ways, we've already answered that. I think that it is fear. This belief that there's not enough, that somehow yours is going to get taken away. So I do believe in the innate goodness of people. And if they're unconstrained, they are going to act in responsible and civil ways. But if they are fearful, and carry a lot of burdens, they're going to begin to oppress.

DAVID: Even to the degree of a Hitler, a Pol Pot, or our own country terms of civil rights?

ANN: Absolutely. Absolutely. And this really, I think, is a driving force—this white supremacy culture, in which is more is better. And I've got to take what's mine because there's scarcity.

DAVID: And that we're better than.

ANN: And we're better than.

> (**Note:** I believe with my entire being the experience of feeling and believing we are "better than" another person, group or culture is an incredibly important aspect of oppression, subjugation, prejudice, and racism. If a person, group or culture is "better than" the other, then the other has to be "less than". A significant aspect to distort a universal truth is the use of Cognitive Physio Mechanisms described in Chapter 7—specifically justification. The mechanism of justification takes a person, group, or culture and objectifies them, severs connections, erodes empathy and compassion, and dissipates our curiosity and then evokes the reason was for the greater good, God, etc. Whenever a part of us utilizes justification in this way, *almost always*, somebody or something comes out as *less than*.)

DAVID: I am interested in your take on this subject too, because I've also grappled with it when someone says to me, "Well, you're white, and you have white privilege".

ANN: Well, it's really about first impressions. Okay? If someone looks at you, the first two things are these: they're going to see that you're male.

Or they might see that you're white, and you're male. Those are the first impressions. So with that, comes a level of privilege. Just on first impressions, and with that comes a level of power.

DAVID: That's something I really want to look at inside because there's a part of me that says, *It didn't seem like too much privilege when my grandparents came here (from Portugal and Italy) with just a suitcase.* And I totally get that we weren't stolen from our country and enslaved and our family systems and culture decimated. [I realize how absurd it is for me to say, "I totally get that." I can't possibly 'get' it! I've got some work to do!] But when I think of those things, it doesn't feel like privilege to me.

ANN: Right. And, it's all on the continuum. It didn't feel like privilege, or it's poverty and there was loss in it. But the fact is that if they even had a suitcase to come here, even if it was just one for five people, it was a level of privilege.

DAVID: Yes, not chained to a galley on a ship or some other horrific experiences.

ANN: What we're learning is that many people of color often don't want to hear about our suffering. They find that disrespectful. We go because we want to join or not feel guilt. *Let me tell you where my family came from so you know we suffered.* But that's like the biggest no-no there is.

DAVID: I will make a special note.

ANN: Because we all step in it, and then we're like *shit*. No.

ANN: Well, I was thinking, I don't believe in evil, per se. I believe evil is when anybody makes somebody else fear love.

DAVID: Say that again.

ANN: I feel like evil is when anyone makes someone else fear love. So, I think that it's the things that you do that make people not be able to trust and feel love, and feel respected, and [deny] their basic human dignity.

DAVID: So how do you see working with legacy burdens addressing some of these things?

ANN: It's a must. You have to become aware of your legacy burdens so that you can unburden them, because they're like veils that you're looking at people in the world through, distorting your perception and constraining you from acting responsibly.

DAVID: A major concept in IFS is to be a hope merchant. So what do you hope for: for yourself, for people, for our country, for our world?

ANN: Well, I'm going to tell you the first thing that came into my head, which is I hope that for myself there is always a deeper spiritual connection. One of my favorite tea bag sayings is "we're spiritual beings having a human experience, and that that spiritual connection is what we need to get us out of this mess we're in, and when you're spiritually connected, you know that we're all connected". And I think that in some ways, that's the message of this COVID thing. There's so much collective grief and coming together to figure it out, with both positives and negatives, and collective anxiety, and collective suffering. It really makes us see that we are a world community and we can interchange Self with Spirit because they feel one and the same to me. So the more Self-leadership I have in my parts, the more connected I am because my definition of spirituality is connection. Connection to myself, connection to others, connection to the planet. That would be my hope for myself and everybody else—that we heal from shame, so that we can be more connected.

Rina Dubin, Ed.D.

Dr. Rina Dubin was the Assistant Trainer during my Level 1 IFS training. It was apparent to the participants that she was incredibly competent at taking care of the myriad of logistics to have the multiple training weekends run smoothly. During the year-long training, the Senior Trainers (Ann Sinko, LMFT and Mike Elkin, LMFT) would participate in a demo with one of the attendees on Friday and Saturday. Ann or Mike would sit in the middle of the room, encircled by all the Program Assistants and about thirty-five participants, and would work with a volunteer's choice of topic or part. I waited until about week four—until I felt confident enough regarding the skills of the Senior Trainers, and the relative safety of potentially sharing something personal with the participants, before I was willing to even think about volunteering. I felt increasingly connected to Ann during the first three weeks, and decided to wait for her turn doing the demo. So, when it was time for the demo on week four, I put my name on a small piece of paper, and put it in the cup along with all the other volunteers. Mike Elkin came by my seat and said, "You're up."

"Up for what?" I asked. "I already put my name in the cup!"

Mike said, "Up for the demo."

I was not nearly as enthusiastic as before, and even less so when, instead of Ann, I saw Rina sitting in the therapist chair. I really thought about saying, "I have reconsidered" or, "It's not the right time for me." Instead, I continued walking and sat in the chair across from Rina. *I have never regretted that decision.* The content of our work included some really tough times when our youngest daughter, Christina, was diagnosed with Type I Diabetes at age two. During that demo, for me, IFS was transformed from the theoretical to the experiential. After that experience, I did not just understand IFS intellectually, I FELT it! I will always be grateful to Rina, and also thankful for my faulty hearing, fate, luck or whatever it was that enabled me to be chosen that day. Thank you, Rina.

DAVID: What I'd like to do is to explore some of the constructs of responsibility, accountability, and civility. So, from a personal perspective, how would you define responsibility?

RINA: My personal responsibility?

Appendix B: Interviews with Ann Sinko, Rina Dubin & Michael Elkin

DAVID: Well, first how would you personally define responsibility, because sometimes there can be a difference between how someone might define responsibility personally, as compared to through an IFS lens.

RINA: More will probably come to me as we talk, But, [I would define it as] being responsible for my impact. I'm thinking more relationally when you talk about responsibility; it's different than the paying-my-bills kind of responsibility.

DAVID: Yes. Can I share the definition I am using? On a more rudimentary level, I define it as knowing the difference for oneself between right and wrong.

RINA: Well, that gets complicated because things are so contextual.

DAVID: Exactly. Exactly! And that therein lies some of the challenge of the book. To not make it judgy and/or black and white, because it is not. I do believe that there are some underpinnings—such as the universal truths: "Do unto others", and the Principle of Dignity and Respect.

RINA: So, where I went to when you said all that about right and wrong, is what goes toward the ultimate greater good. Because you know that what's considered *wrong* can be parsed out differently in different contexts. So I guess it made me think about what's for the greater good, and the responsibility for that.

DAVID: From an IFS perspective, would you define it in the same way? Or would it be different?

RINA: No, I think it's pretty much the same. It [IFS] just gives us more tools to parse it out. We start to develop a felt sense of when we would be making a decision from a reactive place (a part), or making a decision from another perspective when we are in a clear, calm space (Self), and can come to clarity about the best approach or resolution. So I think in that way, IFS gives us a different filter to sort through it.

DAVID: Could you speak to what a protector does for those not familiar with IFS, and talk a little bit about what it's like to be driven by a protector?

RINA: Well, it would mean that I'm in some kind of action to make something feel better inside of me. Now, doing good in general can make us feel good, but a protector's job is to try to make something feel better that's not feeling good. Like, I'll be a better person, or I'll be better liked, or people will think more of me. So, that would be more parts-driven.

DAVID: Why do you feel some people who appear to be Self-led, abandon responsibility?

RINA: Do you want to give an example of that?

> *After a fairly long pause I realize that Rina has gently pointed out a part-driven question. My question assumes someone can be Self-led all the time, and that's not possible.*

DAVID: Ahhh, because nobody is Self-led all the time?

RINA: That's correct. So I could abandon responsibility in one case, and then in many other ways be Self-led... except when I'm not. Because when our parts are activated, which we all have, we're no longer Self-led. So that's what takes us out of Self- leadership, if you will—or being Self-led, is activated parts. And the scan (a scan is like using a radar system on our internal system) gives us a way of tracking (following what is happening) so that we can learn more about our systems' way of tracking as well. So I can say later, "Oh, I don't think I made a decision from the most clear place". You know, like maybe I'm really angry at somebody and I decided to end the relationship. But in another moment, I might have a different view of the value of that, and I just got so angry with that person that I ended the relationship. That's it.

DAVID: So maybe a better way to phrase that question would be: Why do we all, or why do parts, lose their sense of responsibility? Something akin to that?

RINA: Yes, parts. So meaning that's part [an aspect of] of our humanity, because none of us can escape that. In addition, protector energy either sees the problem outside and goes into blame, or judges something [a part] inside- and also goes into blame.

DAVID: I guess a part wrote that question.

RINA: Now, am I the first person to say this to you about that question?

DAVID: I think so...

RINA: I'm interested in the other answers, because I can't see another answer about what takes us out of being Self-led, which is parts.

DAVID: Well, I think that's been a consistent response about what takes us out of being Self-led, which is parts, but you are the first to question the word "some." That would be, as you say, a trailhead [for me].

RINA: The word some?

DAVID: Yes. Rather than, we all stray from that.

RINA: Yes, because we all have parts. Parts are facets of our humanity, and our challenge of being human.

DAVID: Very good. So, the next question, from your personal perspective, would be: How would you define civility?

RINA: It feels like a sense of decency, a sense of respect, and some sense of "Do unto others", and it sort of has kindness woven into it.

DAVID: And from an IFS perspective, would it be the same or different?

RINA: So, I don't know that anything's going to be different. Again, I think IFS extends a technology or a mechanism for working it better, and brings in some civility because they ultimately ask us to bring kindness to our own [parts] hearts when they're activated.

So it feels like it gives us a path for what to do when we are not in civility, and we're in a part(s).

DAVID: Thank you. How would you define accountability?

RINA: Well, it's connected to responsibility—it has a sort of taking ownership aspect. I know in AA they talk about cleaning up my side of the street. I mean, if I'm in a tangle with somebody, then I can slow down and eventually get clear about what my contribution to that tangle was. And then, being accountable would be willing to probably say it out loud to the other person. First I have to find it myself. But then if I'm really putting it out there into the community—or in this case, to another person. My willingness to say, *you know, I can see where I got caught in that and I'm sorry, or I will work on that.* So, it sits pretty close with responsibility in a lot of ways. [This is a wonderful example of the process of Internal Accountability, responsibility, and what a Self-led apology would sound like in Chapter 12.]

DAVID: Yes, it's included in one of the definitions I use for responsibility: to be answerable, to be accountable.

RINA: Yes. So answerable meaning, *not* so I can beat myself up or get my sixty lashes or whatever. But I like that piece about cleaning up my side of the street. That's what I have potential control over. I don't really have control over what you or someone else does.

DAVID: Do you feel a standard of responsibility and civility has eroded over time in our country and our world?

RINA: Well, it's complicated the way I see it, because I'm a little older than you. When I was growing up, there was a sort of an automatic deference to authority, which I thought was really problematic: "because the teacher said so", "because the principal", "because the cop". Then automatically, we were supposed to have a certain deference to that and to authority, and that didn't sit well. And I think a lot of that got challenged in the '60s, which certainly is when I came of age. And I was really glad for that. But I think then it becomes a slippery slope anything goes. And in this particular era we're in, under our current leadership, and the discontent that shows in this polarizing, aggressive way, it's gotten much worse.

DAVID: I concur. Do you believe our leaders have an impact on how citizens embrace or reject responsibility and civility?

RINA: Yes. Absolutely. Because, things dribble down from the top and when we have this blaming, it's not right/wrong in the way you meant it, but blaming [in the sense of] "those are bad people", and scapegoating, and all of that. That's the kind of leadership we're in and it's very, very satisfying, temporarily, to blame. But it doesn't lead to those other things you're talking about, which I think makes for a much more civil and decent culture.

DAVID: Do you believe in the innate good in people? And if so, how do you grapple with the fact that human beings—often men—continue to oppress and subjugate?

RINA: Yes, I do. But I also believe as humans we get threatened and scared by losing out, and then we become tribal and in fear of the other, and that fear is also wired into us. And so, it's not one or the other. We can live in a culture where it feels like there's not enough, and then we get into *us* and *them*, and then there's this drive for power. And in our country, and we are not the only one, there's also a lot of power tied to money, which sets up a whole chain of those who have power over those with less financial resources: the haves and have-nots. There's a lot of jockeying for who's got resources and how to hold onto them, and make sure they're ours and not somebody else's. So there's a lot of that and *that's not good*.

DAVID: And do you have any thoughts about why men continue to be so oppressive? In so many cultures throughout time?

RINA: You're talking about a gender thing now?

DAVID: Yes.

RINA: Well, that's a complicated question.

DAVID: I agree.

RINA: What's good about testosterone wiring? And this is a generalization, but men live in a different biology in that way. I'm sure that had some function when we were early on in civilization. But, yes, that's complicated about why men oppress. I mean, because they can, I suppose, because they've been, and physically, might makes right. And, if I want to strip it down more, men and women are somewhat wired differently about sexuality. There's a lot about power over, if we are talking about men's power over women.

DAVID: Yes, and one thing I used to talk about in Domestic Violence Groups is not only the physical disparity, but something in the wiring. I call it "the willingness to harm." And throughout time, men have been more willing to harm than women.

RINA: And what would make it that way?

DAVID: Yes.

RINA: What's innate? What's innate in that? What's socialized in that? And I don't have the answer for that. But, because we grew up in the culture we did that was socialized into us, we don't really know its essence. I'm not saying it's not wired in some other biological way. But it's also been socialized so deeply in our culture. If you look at some aborigine cultures, they vary. Some of them are very aggressive, and some of them are very gentle. How do we explain that, because they have men and women in those cultures? Also, what happened when some of the original cultures were female-led? That's mostly it, except maybe for a few little islands somewhere, that's mostly gone away. Because I suppose ideally there'd be a balance, and that's not what we have.

DAVID: And that's the essence of the Tai Chi symbol, which is the *balance* between Yin and Yang—those universal principles, and all the vacillations in between.

RINA: Yes, it's not in balance.

RINA: No. So I mean, in order to harm over, I think there's a certain level, and I don't know what it's like living inside of a man's body, but there's a certain level of dissociation that has to happen to hurt another human being. (Note: If this intrigues you please look up the work of Lt. Col. Dave Grossman.) And I see that racially too, as there has to be the *other;* that's not human the way I am. Otherwise, I couldn't do that.

DAVID: I do spend a fair amount of time talking about the mechanisms which facilitate that kind of ability or willingness.

RINA: So you're going into all that stuff around the gender templates.

DAVID: It's not the main piece of it, but it is a part of it, and I feel it needs to be a part of it. Because, there's a lot of things that are happening in our country now, where men are leading this imbalance.

RINA: And with patriarchy even if it's not men per se, the dominant patriarchy values are in all of us, and some of them are quite toxic. Just like white privilege is toxic. But it's in all of us, and even in people of color. There's white privilege stuff or there's patriarchy. I carry that, and it dehumanizes me.

DAVID: How so?

RINA: Well, because if I'm a gay person, I've picked up homophobia, so I have parts of me that will feel I'm less than. Can I now have some misogyny in me that says, "Well you really should hang back", or "You don't want to be a threat", or "You don't want to be seen as a bitch". No, that's me having swallowed the patriarchy we live in. When I'm with some men I can sense how they feel more entitled to certain things [and they believe] they should have this privilege because they're men. They take up more space, or they touch people who don't necessarily want to be touched—those kinds of things. So, we've internalized that stuff, even if we think we're not that, or we're not that color, or we're not that gender—we've still internalized the same stuff.

(**Note:** After Dr. (Dick) Schwartz's suggestion, and Dr. (Rina) Dubin's interview and input, I purchased *Soul on Ice* by Eldridge Cleaver. He provides an accounting of this internalization Dr. Dubin is referring to about a billion times more powerfully and poignantly than I could, especially on pages 28-35. Mr. Cleaver describes an internalization which he has recognized as: "a black growing up in America is indoctrinated with the white race's standard of beauty." Mr. Cleaver goes on to write about how torturous (and the word we would use in IFS is polarizing) those—and so many other—indoctrinations, were and are.)

DAVID: Yes. So lastly, a major concept in IFS is to be a hope merchant. What do you hope for—for yourself, for people, for our country, and for the world?

RINA: Well, I think one of the reasons I've been involved in trainings as much as I have is because I'm hoping to get this way of living in our own systems, and living in larger systems, more out there. So meaning that, being able to track and notice, and being mindful enough to notice our reactivity, or being open if someone else notices it—because sometimes we don't see it. Like when Mike talks about the spinach on your teeth [another Mikeism!]—that makes for a more civil, accountable world. So

Appendix B: Interviews with Ann Sinko, Rina Dubin & Michael Elkin

again, that's been a good fit for me because it's not just about what happens in my office. It's that thing about IFS; it's not just a therapy model—it's a way of living that we bring everywhere. That doesn't mean I do it well everywhere. I'm not saying that, but that's the practice or the intention. Like you've taken your Tai Chi into your world, even though you're not literally doing the movements. You have a lot of that you take with you, right?

DAVID: Yes. And now a lot of IFS as well.

RINA: Well, they marry very well.

DAVID: Very, very well.

RINA: And you have those things on a body level that you've married with IFS.

DAVID: Yes. So what do you hope for in our country?

RINA: Well, I hope for leadership which I see little of. Well, there are a bunch of things—if I get into my political views—there are a bunch of things I see as connected. I think the media has been compromised ever since money got involved, with the sound bites and what's sexy news, or sensational news. We don't have any Walter Cronkites anymore. So that erosion has just happened in our lifetime, and it has made that much worse, obviously, in the last three and a half years. By fake news and mistrust [that engenders] that much more mistrust. I think the media has really been in a very jaundiced place, and that allows other things to happen and then again, people protecting interests that have to do with their own. To your point about what is civil and what's just, [as compared to people] protecting their own selfish needs and not what's for the greater good. So now what does that mean about our other party starting to have enough traction and enough leadership, because it's wobbly? So that's what I hope for. But you know, so far, it's not that impressive. I don't know what that's all about, except that we're in some horrible fascist slide that's now exploding. I can hope that good comes out of this because this system may well crash and burn.

DAVID: And as I watched things like when the speaker Nancy Pelosi was ripping up Trump's speech at the end of that presidential address, and I remember how you and Michael would talk about how protectors energize other people's protectors. I thought, "Oh my goodness, there they are". They [Speaker Pelosi and President Trump's parts] are absolutely polarized, both not behaving well, and I felt they were absolutely blended with those parts.

RINA: I do think Nancy Pelosi was trying to protest—which I support—and yet it leaned into a way that was going to land as disrespectful to the other side of the equation, right? So how do you protest in a dignified way, because she also was saying "this isn't okay", and she's right. So, I don't know what I would have done in that moment. I can understand that frustration. I understand your point that it alienates people who see it as disrespectful.

DAVID: Yes, and to me, it was so apparent that it's not black-and-white [Pelosi and Trump]. Now with the civil rights protests, how do you even know now with everything that's going on? How do you protest? In which way do you protest? Where does it go? There are people using the protests for something that has nothing to do with the injustices and inequalities, and there are people who *are* protesting that very thing.

RINA: Well, and even the language—because people are calling it riots, and it's not a riot, it's a protest. To your point, there may be people rioting that are just into being destructive, but most of the people that are out there are not rioting—they are protesting. And if we bring curiosity to why someone would want to "just riot," we are going to get to exiles that have been wounded and feel hopeless and frustrated.

DAVID: Yes. Which is different.

Appendix B: Interviews with Ann Sinko, Rina Dubin & Michael Elkin

RINA: It is. Yes

DAVID: Thanks. Even if people like President Trump and other people had a starting point like the rudimentary definition of civility, and there was a core fuel underneath, it could be a starting point.

RINA: Yet, we have to be willing to look at our own contribution too.

DAVID: Yes. But if people were civil and polite in a perfunctory manner, I believe that would be a substantial improvement. [I have reevaluated this last statement.]

RINA: Well, perhaps. I had a thing [an interaction] on a staff because someone used the word polite and other people heard judgment in it and were asking, "Are you saying I'm being impolite?" So that was just a whole little side thing, because I think polite can sound like we are constrained and restrained, rather than how we can have some difficult conversations and still hold respect and the ability to listen.

DAVID: That is something which will be included in an additional definition of civility that you, Richard, and Ann have all spoken about. Arguably, civility could be on a much more rudimentary level, but it's not anything that we really want to aim for—not the ultimate goal.

(**Note:** A part of me initially braced up against Rina's example of polite, mainly because a part of me questioned the original definition I used. However, later I began to work with my stuff and came to some conclusions. After Rina's example and insight, I still believe being polite could be better than what we have now. However, polite can also be delivered in a similar way to the duality of pity. Polite can be just that, but if the core fuel is disgust, distaste, and/or contempt, that message too, can and is delivered loud and clear as well. (Rina's ability to illuminate something like this is not unfamiliar. Thank you, Rina!)

RINA: Value and respect has some hard energy. It's not just this intellectual concept, because then I think it falls short.

DAVID: That's not how I would think of it. It has to have that emotional content.

RINA: Right. Exactly. It makes me think about religious institutions, which I haven't really grown up in—but you know which ones, and talking about the media, which ones are really walking the walk about the other, the person who's not my faith or not my color, versus these platitudes that people get taught, that they don't don't really act, and then they don't really bring (these qualities) into their lives. Yes, piousness—but no practice really.

DAVID: What's the definition of piousness? I kind of know, but I don't.

RINA: I guess I want to say, it has a righteousness to it.

DAVID: It's kind of like talking the talk, but you don't walk the walk. Kind of like pity.

RINA: Like, holier than, "I've got the right way, but meanwhile, I do what I want to do and I'm judging you. And I'm not checking my own. I'm above it somehow".

Michael Elkin, LMFT

Michael is a master of making a connection, and maintaining that connection throughout the entire therapeutic session with volunteers in the IFS trainings, and his clients in private practice. In a conversation with Michael, I told him he is like a Tai Chi Master; once he has sat down with a volunteer for a demo, or a client for a session, he is able to follow a person, and their parts, wherever they may go—without losing the connection no matter how difficult the process is going. In addition, he is able to do this

Appendix B: Interviews with Ann Sinko, Rina Dubin & Michael Elkin

while being respectful, civil, curious, and compassionate to the other person's parts and internal system. The only way to do this consistently is to have done an enormous amount of personal work to understand your parts and Self. Michael has exceeded that requirement and more.

I would be remiss if I did not mention that Michael, in addition to his extraordinary skills, often shares what we as participants and trainers have come to call "Mike-isms." A brief example: Michael, Ann, and Rina were leading an IFS training during which I was a program assistant—which is like a teaching assistant. I had just facilitated a group exercise and it did not go well. I was lamenting about what a poor job I did and was looking for feedback. Michael said, "David, despite your efforts, perfection will continue to elude you." Note to reader: almost all Mikeisms are followed by Mike's deep, hearty laugh, in conjunction with his shoulders going up and down, and a, "Heh, Heh Heh, Heh" by Michael himself. Mike-isms are short nuggets of wisdom and universal truths that resonate in most, if not all of us; and it is his openness, heart, and compassion that touches us.

DAVID: I believe Internal Family Systems (IFS) can be a way to reconnect with responsibility, accountability, and civility, so I'd like to explore these concepts with you. And I'm especially curious about your thoughts on morals and the moral meaning given this subject matter.

For instance, when you say, "There is no moral meaning being in a part or self", I find it particularly intriguing because I am postulating that principles, like the principle of responsibility, can't be reduced to a black and white, either/or version of right and wrong. However, I do believe there are basic foundational underpinnings of moral and universal truths. And in addition, these types of situations require a contextual framework as well.

So, from your personal perspective, how would you define responsibility?

MIKE: Well, if it's okay with you, I'm going to answer that starting with a story. I learned about responsibility from a guy who's a very talented hypnotherapist who had the confidence of my mentor. And I found out he turned out to be a scumbag, and he was screwing his clients. And he and I had had a bigger, you know, a frank *exchange* of views about that. But back before I found out, he just said, "Look, responsibility is a simple word, and it's different from blame, and it's different from obligation. It means the ability to respond, you can respond".

DAVID: So what does that mean?

MIKE: Well, what it means is that you're putting up—you're dealing with a situation in which your parts are configured in such a way that you're able to respond because there are no energized parts preventing you from responding in a useful way. And so it is with IFS. Because what one of the things IFS does is make complex things simple and simple things complex. So, it's like a person can be responsible to deal with a situation one minute, and not responsible the next minute, because some part gets triggered and jumps them, and blocks his access, to say, his linear intellect. And he gets all mad, or he gets hurt, or he gets distracted, and then he's not responsible. Does that make him bad? No. Does that make him undependable? Yes.

And, the amount of work people have done with their parts, the more likely it is that they're not going to get triggered. And the more likely it is they'll be able to be responsible more of the time, and respond to situations in a useful way, and be able to do what their best understanding thinks is appropriate.

So, that's my view of responsibility, which I would guess is probably consistent with most IFS thinking.

DAVID: Yes, that's becoming a familiar theme in the interviews, that responsibility is this ability to respond, and what you added as well.

MIKE: Yes, I teach that in Level 1 because I do want to make the distinctions between blame, obligation, and responsibility because they're all very different words.

DAVID: So, would you say your view of responsibility is the same as IFS?

MIKE: It's the same as through an IFS lens. They're one and the same. Ah, well, I see what you're setting up. I have two major lenses, and one is *A Course in Miracles*, and the other is IFS. And they're pretty consistent. There's a couple of tiny variants, but that's my lens. That's my paradigm for understanding the mind and human functioning, and I think it's pretty consistent. I don't think I would get the big arguments with any of my IFS colleagues about that. I don't know. I wouldn't anticipate any shit.

DAVID: (laughing) Okay, it seems like you've answered this question before, but one of the questions I had is: Why do people who appear to be Self-led, then sometimes abandon their sense of responsibility?

MIKE: Yes, well right, because they get hijacked. There are some very well-known people [in the world of psychology] who are famous for getting hijacked when people challenge them. Even though they have done a lot of work, and use the model as well as anybody, they've still got their parts. My teacher for *A Course in Miracles*, Ken Wapnick, was about the most Self-led person I've ever been in the presence of for any length of time. I've seen some people [do it] for like, ten minutes. But because I know him well enough, I knew where his triggers were at. He could [still] go from parts to Self-led. However, he actually wound up suing a person to sign an agreement that would say they would not teach *A Course in Miracles*. So, Self doesn't get into lawsuits. I just gotta say, that's protector energy. It sort of amplifies. So, we human beings are not the predictable beings that we try to be, and if I know somebody well enough, and I know something about their triggers, I think I can predict pretty well when they'd be responsible and dependable, and when you just move around them because they're not going to be an asset.

DAVID: So, from both your personal and IFS perspective, how would you define civility?

MIKE: Well, the thing is, one of my major mentors is a woman named Judith Martin, who writes under the name Miss Manners. George Bernard Shaw said, "If you're going to tell the truth, better make it funny". And she does.

But what she says is [that] human life goes better when people treat each other with respect, and she doesn't put the word in—but I do—*curiosity*. Which means you don't assume you know the meaning of something until you have made an inquiry. And then we assign meaning to it.

So, it's basically avoiding and reacting to situations with protector energy. Because my protectors don't have curiosity, they are also not responding to what's going on out there. They're responding to what's going on in here (Michael points to inside his body). So they're very unlikely to act in a way consistent with my wellbeing, or the wellbeing of others. So civility is basically keeping your protector energy to the absolute minimum. The way to do that is, we try to heal the parts that trigger them because once they're triggered, they do their thing. I could get hit somewhere (Mike's points to inside his body again), and my IQ goes down like seventy points. And I'm not civil; I'm impatient.

I [would] see people as basically in relation to meet my needs. If I'm narcissistic, [I would ask] "What have you done for me lately?" And so, it's my goal to be able to be civil with everybody. And yesterday, I had a conversation with my granddaughter who had been held hostage by my daughter-in-law for over two years. And my daughter-in-law was there, and I was able to be civil. I was able to just—I was polite. (Note: Michael's description sounds like it's in the same ballpark as the more basic definition of civil, and makes sense in this context.) I did not pursue a conversation with her. But I did my best to not convey hostility, contempt, or judgment, and it's hard to do because we are always communicating with parts that we don't know we are communicating with. You know, how many times have you heard somebody say, "I'M NOT ANGRY!"

And they believe that, they absolutely do. Nobody else does. But they do, because they were not aware of that part communicating, and you know this right? (Michael pulls the side of his lip up, like a sneer.) It's a universal expression of contempt. I think it explains often why people say, "Hey! what did I say??" (in an exasperated way), and they don't know they did that, but the other person does. And if they didn't know, [what that expression means] whether that person just came back from a tribe that has had no contact with the outside world, or your next door neighbor, that means contempt to humans. And very often, people don't know they've done it.

So, if somebody, for instance, reacts to you with hostility, it's really useful to get curious about it because it's likely it was triggered by some communication of yours.

And therefore, if they're feeling defensive, they feel attacked. And it's useful if you can keep *your* protectors down to find out why they voted, and attacked, and what their experience was.

DAVID: And you're saying about it? Protector energy attracts other protectors?

MIKE: What I say is [that] protectors never protect. What they do invariably, is they energize and attract that which they protect against.

And a really simple demonstration of this is by saying, [now in a stern voice] "You KNOW DAVID, I don't feel respected. I need MORE respect". And then I just ask, "David, do you respect me more or less than you did 10 seconds ago?" Heh Heh Heh Heh! And then anything you might say after that, like a defensive reaction, then I'll send [my part] more troops and dig a little deeper. "Really David, *Dooo YOU RESPECT MEEEE*"? So yes, that's what protectors do, or whether they're police departments as we see now. What is their stated goal? To restore order.

But protectors put out the fire with gasoline; that's what they're doing. There was a cartoon in *The Globe* yesterday or the day before with Trump putting out COVID with with gasoline. So this is not a brand new analogy on my part but yes, protector energy is to be avoided.

My protectors and your protectors, they all act pretty much the same. They see the world in black and white, us and them, always and never. They have been forced to do extreme roles, and they do not serve us; they do not enhance the quality of our lives. So the less they act in me, the better my life is going to go.

DAVID: So for those parts that have been forced into extreme roles, then their experience is to react in a similar way.

MIKE: Yes, they're there. They get into fights and neither of us has won a fight. I don't think you've ever talked to anybody who's won a fight, so the fewer you get into, the better off.

DAVID: Thank you. How would you define accountability?

MIKE: Well, you know, there's another story there. My son, when he was younger, was a music prodigy, and so when he was about fifteen, he was playing with guys much older. There was this one guy named Vinny. Vinny was a very talented musician, who, my guess, was brought up feral.

So he'd say, "I'll come over and we will rehearse", and he wouldn't. He'd borrow instruments and sell them. He didn't have a driver's license, and one day I had to drive him somewhere. And he was saying, "Your son is to blame for the fact that he is pissed off at me because I don't come to all the rehearsals". And I said, "Vinny, I'm actually grateful to you for the way you're dealing with my son because basically", [and I didn't use parts], "I divide the world into two groups of people: the people who do what they say they're gonna do, and the people who don't do what they say they're gonna do—and I treat both of those groups very differently. My son is fifteen and he doesn't yet know how to deal effectively with people who don't do what they say they're gonna do. And you're teaching him, and I don't think you've harmed him in any way, and I have no animosity toward you. I'm concerned for you, because the way you're behaving, your life is going to go in a way that you really aren't going to want it to go."

He doesn't understand human interaction, which is, the way we can feel safe around each other with contracts. Like you said, "Hey, I'll talk to you at 11 o'clock". And I said, "Fine". And so you had every reasonable belief that I would be available at 11 o'clock. And if I weren't, given our relationship, you would assume that something horrible happened to me. Because you have reason to believe I'm going to do what I say. And so you treat me in a way consistent with that. Like, "if Mike agrees to be interviewed, I expect when we set it up, he's gonna interview with me and do his best". Or, if you have a few experiences where I don't do what I say I'm going to do, then the space between us becomes less safe because it's going to be painful for me to deal with you, because it would be like, "How do I know I'm racist? Because when I see a black person, I feel shame". A black friend visited yesterday. And I told him it was nice to see him. And now that the shit is hitting the fan, I've really been thinking about my racial attitudes. I also feel shame when I see him, because I'm part of a group that has benefited from racism. I live in a different country than his [his friend lives in the U.S.], and we hold him accountable for being a full citizen without letting him be a full citizen. We had a good discussion.

It's a very funny term, accountability, because it's a contractual thing. And for instance, the criminal justice system in white America holds black people accountable to a standard that's not appropriate, and isn't part of the contract. They didn't contract and we imposed this on them. And we have a history of doing that with people with unfashionable complexions.

So it's a funny word—accountability—it engenders a feeling of safety. And because there are two emotions, love and fear, and the presence of fear blocks the awareness of love, which means that when our relationship doesn't feel safe—even if we love each other—we're not going to feel that love. We are going to feel shame or threat. Whereas the threat is, the threat of shame. Like if I turned my computer on to be interviewed, and you stood me up, then [I wonder] "where's David?"

DAVID: Ah.

MIKE: My parts will think it's about me. And you might think I'm not worth the time and effort. And I have parts that will give you the ability to determine my worth, and then you project my judging parts out on you, and you become dangerous to me. And then basically, Self-energy is not available to us. Because I'm going to be in protector energy and parts.

Again, accountability, the way I look at it, is basically if people's parts will allow them to keep contracts, then the interactions between them can become safer and more and more Self-led. And relationships get more and more useful to people.

MIKE: Yes. I had a therapist-mentor named Dick Chasen, who was a psychiatrist in Cambridge. He was one of the most important people I've ever met; he was the kind of guy that if the head of Mass General needed a psychiatrist, they would call Dick. He was that kind of guy. And he was married to Laura Chasen who started the Public Conversation Project. And her maiden name was Rockefeller; she was David's daughter.

MIKE: He was good and he said, "If you're having trouble with a client, check the contract". It's always the contract. Later, I can understand it's always my parts. And a part of mine might have fucked up the contract, Heh heh heh, or is currently fucking up the contract. But he (Dick Chasen) would say contract, contract, contract.

MIKE: And I just started a new consultation group and I let them know I'm going to be really stressing contract, and if you think about that, before you present or you think about your cases through that lens, I'll probably be more useful to you.

DAVID: Yes, contracting—it's essential. I have like a semi David-ism story. When I am providing consultation and they are having difficulty I may say, I often have the voice of my dear teacher and mentor Mike Elkin in my head. Usually it's comforting. Sometimes it's a little distressing. However, when he provides consultation for me, there will always be a question regarding "what's your contract?" And almost every time I've come to him for supervision, and I've been stuck, the culprit is that I don't have a contract, or I've drifted away from that.

MIKE: It was amazing how that learning was for that one thing, and you started really asking, "What is our contract?" And I don't remember having to talk to you much after that. You got it.

DAVID: Do you believe that a standard of responsibility and civility has eroded over time in our country, in the world. And what might you attribute this to?

MIKE: See, it's hard to know, I'll tell you. I say it's hard to be optimistic, and I see everything turning to shit, but when you're seventy-eight years old, that's your job to say, "What the fuck? Everything turned to shit." Back in the good old days when we had Jim Crow laws. The Korean War. You know, America was *great* back then.

But, Max, my oldest son, has a fifteen-year-old daughter, so fate has a hostage with him. Even though I have parts that think of him as having a sort of gloomy view, being a father is central to his identity. And he's optimistic, and he's saying, "Look, you say everything's going to shit. In your lifetime, the concept of human rights was not a concept, it was not something people thought about".

And it's true. I mean, we both are old enough to have gone to the south and seen segregated bathrooms. The idea of human rights was not a concept, and now—it's an important concept. The idea of women being treated as human beings did not exist when I was an adult. Now, just in my lifetime, it's a very important concept.

And my son said, and this is a thing I find less comforting—our access to controlling our environment or technology is increasing exponentially. And we'll think of a way around this. That—I'm less convinced of. But, God bless him.

Do I think people are more or less civil than they were? I think Trump is an expression of the fact that people were so scared, and then they stopped pretending to basically be who they are told who they should be. And they just are much more likely to act out fearful projectors because they have permission to, and there is a sense of relief when you can see your problems as being the fault of others, like with the Muslims, the Mexicans, and now it's the Chinese that are responsible for our pain (due to COVID-19). And when you do that, first of all, you lose responsibility. For instance, the Chinese are gonna have to fix this, it's theirs, and I'm waiting for them to just straighten the whole thing out. Well, what can I do? I'm a helpless victim. I'm not responsible.

DAVID: So that ties into the next question which is: Do you believe our leaders have an impact on how citizens embrace or reject responsibility, accountability, and civility?

MIKE: I mean, he got elected. Now, he didn't win a majority, but he got elected. And then, I don't think happily of his way of responding to COVID and the police murders. I think that may in fact, prevent him from getting reelected. But I would have bet money he would get reelected before COVID hit. Which means, it's not like it's subtle who he is, and what he believes. He's not deceptive. He's a liar, but he deceives no one. I mean, everybody who votes for or supports him knows what he is, and they're supporting and endorsing those parts of their protective system that he expresses, embodies, and supports. So it's a cybernetic process. I mean, he just could be an asshole with a TV show and lawsuits, because apparently you don't want to do business with this guy.

But we've elevated him to the most destructive being in the world right now. And he's not a bad guy. He can't help it. You know, as a matter of fact, another thing I just finished writing is why Donald Trump isn't a bad person. He's certainly not where I want him. He's certainly the most *dangerous* person in the world right now.

But, he didn't get there by accident. So it's cybernetic we elected him and then he reinforces the fears that got elected in the first place. So I guess the thing is, we didn't act very well under Obama—who's noble, thoughtful, and articulate. Yes, he's a wonderful human being. But we did not do so good when he was president either, and he had eight years. I think another reason Trump is elected is that people saw this as a cure for Obama.

And he has tried, and made it clear, that he wants to undo everything Obama did. And if he [Obama} could have been killed, he would. Because he is a symbol that people who just shouldn't be in power have gotten way too uppity.

DAVID: There's a thin veil over that.

MIKE: Not anymore. It's gone to tatters. Now, heh heh, the veil is burning.

DAVID: How about when Trump refers to the white nationalists as being included as "fine people"?

MIKE: They're not bad people, but they are people that basically embody

Appendix B: Interviews with Ann Sinko, Rina Dubin & Michael Elkin

very destructive ideas. And they're not bad people. They're no worse than I am. But I don't want to be around them.

DAVID: Do you believe in the innate good in people? And if so, how do you grapple with the fact that human beings—usually men—have continued to oppress and subjugate?

MIKE: Well, of course I believe in the end, who we really are, [is] compassion and curiosity. But, we're also basically evolved from primates. And you know, we have 98% or 99%, of the DNA or something of chimpanzee DNA, and males in most primates, certainly chimpanzees, are very hierarchical. And so that's a very strong thing, the competition among men at the thought of dominance and subjugation in our DNA. And then male sexuality is inherently objectifying and predatory.

And being a guy with [male genitalia], you know what I'm talking about. And, the fact that you are extremely scrupulous about keeping that from causing harm to you and other people. And I have learned that over time and the fact that I'm an old guy, and I'm not pumping out the kind of testosterone I was, say twenty or thirty years ago.

So, testosterone does not generally make us more civil or dependable. So, I'm so gratified hearing from people with Self-led feedback. I've heard from a lot of women say that I'm the first man in power that they felt safe with. But if they knew me forty years ago, they wouldn't have felt safe with me because I would have hit on them.

When I used to run seminars, I slept with the participants of the seminar. This was probably thirty-five to forty years ago. It was more popular then and the thought was, "Hey, everybody does it". But it was a misuse of power, of course. I didn't even know I had privilege. "What? What privilege?" So, that has to be taken into account. And then you got scarcity of goods with scarcity competition, and also I think because being a good person is so central to us. And because women are basically genetically bred to be caretakers and to take the community into account in decision-making, and men aren't.

Women, if you use moral-meaning judgement, women are better than men are.

You know what they say—if you give money to a man, he'll gamble it and spend it on liquor and gambling. And if you give money to a woman, they'll spend it on education and developing the community. And I give a lot of money to this thing called *The Hunger Project* which basically tries to give women economic and political skills. Because the more women run things, the safer we all are. And you and I are miracles of rehabilitation, in that I think both of us are safe for women to be around.

And I don't know about your early life when you were a rock musician; rock musicians are *famous* for being irresponsible in their treatment of women—particularly groupies. I was never violent and I was never coercive, but I was manipulative, predatory and persistent.

DAVID: I relate to that as well.

MIKE: I'm not surprised about that David because you look just like a guy with a [male genitalia]. I'm so grateful that I got a chance to live long enough to get some of my head out of my ass. Because nobody would have bet that I could get this far, given the fact that I was a chain smoker and I gambled with strangers for their money. And I did a lot of things that were unwise and had almost no possibility of working out well for me.

DAVID: Many of the guys from my old band days, when they see me, they say, "You're a therapist? What? **You're** a therapist?"

MIKE: "You're ALIVE??? You've got a family? You went to college?"

DAVID: They can't even imagine.

MIKE: But isn't it like a different life?

DAVID: It is different!

DAVID: So, lastly, a major concept in Internal Family Systems is to be a hope merchant. So, what do you hope for yourself, for our country, and for our world?

Appendix B: Interviews with Ann Sinko, Rina Dubin & Michael Elkin

MIKE: Ah, well for myself, I've got to say I'm more content right now then I have ever been in my life. I'm doing well because the fact that my body isn't working well isn't standing in my way. I got nowhere to go anyway. Heh heh heh. So, I have nine steps from the downstairs to the upstairs. When I get to the top, I'm breathing hard because my lungs are bad enough that I have a handicap tag on my car. That's what it's from. So I've been tested—I have less than a third of my lung capacity. So, I'm just hoping I get to spend as much time with the people I love as I can. And I think a lot of people feel that way because it's been coming at me too. I've been reconnecting with people that I've been way out of touch with, like my friend who called me because his wife is dying. I last saw him and directly dealt with him last summer.

And this guy used to be nasty—he was the best street fighter I knew. I got a chance to see him in action, on several occasions. He was very easy to rile. And now he's just one of the most gentle and loving beings I know. Now we've talked twice—he reached out because he needs a shoulder and he said that. So that's happening. And also my relationship with my kids is healed. And I've reached out and I'm bringing my granddaughter back into my life, and I have forgiven her mother because she has caused me no harm. My granddaughter is an attached being and is available. My son is flourishing, and she's gonna have to figure out some way of dealing with her fear.

But so I'm pretty happy with where I'm at. My wife really believes, from the chair she's sitting in and that holds her, that the planet is doomed, and that in twenty years it will not be able to support human life. That's what she thinks. I really hope that's not true because I also have a granddaughter who is twenty-one months old, and another is fifteen and just waking up, and both of them are really adorable.

But I don't know if they'll have a world to grow up in. And also because the climate stuff is going to create enormous scarcity. I have enormous fear that when certain countries run out of water, they're going to want to take the water from other countries, and they're going to roll across the border with tanks that we have sold [to] them to enhance American prosperity. So my intellect finds it really hard to believe this world is going to go well. The course in miracles tells me it doesn't exist, and it's just a dream, and that it's unwise to take anything that happens here seriously. But that's what we call Level One. Which means that is probably what's real, and it really is a dream, and we probably don't exist, and you and I aren't here—we're just in a dream. But that has nothing to do with my experience, which is you're here, I'm here, I've got my parts and you've got your parts. I get a toothache and it can dominate my experience. So in terms of my intellect, I can't imagine how this earth is going to be able to sustain any type of life that resembles in any way the kind of life I'm living right now.

In fact, I think the pandemic has changed the world; the world you and I are used to, is over. I don't know what the one *is* we're going to be in. Or what the one we are in now is going to be like, but it's probably going to be a lot less convenient. As Jello Biafra said, "Give me convenience or give me death." Heh heh heh!

DAVID: So how do you feel that maybe IFS could play a role and change the course?

MIKE: Well, obviously my embrace of it is because I see it as the most hopeful tool I've run into, that I could use. And I feel privileged I got in contact with it at a point in my career when I was young enough to learn it, master it, and teach it. And because, as a therapy technique, it's certainly the most powerful tool for healing that's been developed. But as a paradigm of mind, it creates options and solutions on a macro basis that weren't there before, and people are really trying to find a way to apply it on a macro basis.

Like for instance: you and Dick. There are books about couples, but you're writing a book about human relationships and paradigm of mind—essentially etiquette. The way people treat each other that's essentially important. And also intrinsically, you're saying, there aren't civil people, or responsible people. There's civility and responsibility, and sometimes it's accessible to us and sometimes it's not.

That's a paradigm, that sort of non-dualistic paradigm that we need to overcome our monkey brains. Cuz, we've run out of time for this shit. Heh Heh Heh Hehh!

Appendix B: Interviews with Ann Sinko, Rina Dubin & Michael Elkin

MIKE: And [organizations like] *Black Therapists Rock* (Deran Young, LCSW) are seeing it as a tool to address racism and to address conflict. It's certainly necessary, and I hope it's sufficient. It is certainly a force for good.

DAVID: I spoke to Deran about being interviewed for the book but she was unable to due to prior commitments and advocacy.

MIKE: Judith [Mike's wife] is an activist. She lies down on train trucks to stop coal trains and things like that. And I don't do that, my demonstration history is not a problem. But, I'm doing my bit. And my bit is I'm trying to spread this way of thinking.

DAVID: And [some] of the major linchpins of this book I use [are] several examples which are kind of mundane; (I give a brief description of the 5 driving scenarios), and really make the distinction between Internal Accountability and External Accountability. And that's a paradigm. The examples of a red traffic light, to go through or not go through.

MIKE: I think of myself as ethical, but not law-abiding. I am a guy who, late at night, will shoot a traffic light without a qualm. Oh, well. (Michael got me, I think I hurt myself laughing so hard.)

DAVID: I include that example as well.

MIKE: Yes. The Internal Accountability is really tough because we're merciless with ourselves. And if we weren't, you and I would be down at the magic mile selling Oldsmobiles. Because the people that we see are functioning the way they are because they have parts that think they're bad.

MIKE: That's what anxiety is: parts that think they're bad, or afraid they're bad. And depression is parts that are sort of locked into the vision of their own badness.

MIKE: And so that's why the moral meaning thing for me is so key. Because we just can't stand being bad; we would rather be in physical pain than in moral pain. If you want, when I get this further along, if you want to see it I'll send it to you.

DAVID: That would be fantastic! Michael, could you repeat your definition of shame.

MIKE: My definition is this: Shame is the experience of having your badness witnessed. Either by judgmental parts of you, or your projections from other people. But, it's still judgemental parts of you.

DAVID: Well, Michael, I can't thank you enough.

APPENDIX C

Education and Leadership

Education and Legacy Burdens

Legacy burdens are burdens we carry from past generations. Again, IFS has a beautiful way to validate, explore, and heal these wounds as well. I have a deep belief and conviction, that until we can more fully address our legacy burdens of racism, we will be doomed to repeat it. We can do it. I believe it will start with the children, especially in regards to education.

It will be a huge undertaking. It would take the magnitude of a tectonic plate shift in how funding is allocated to develop an educational system which benefits all. But it is not only the allocation of funding, but establishing of a foundation and framework for the benefit of children and families, like in the South Bronx, and to be fully educated in a safe environment (as is possible). This is *not* a *No Child Left Behind*, Common Core, *Just say No* (to drugs), Student Learning Objectives—where teachers are required to test each student on the first days of school and predict where they will be at the end of the year, or other programs that cost millions and millions of dollars, sounded great, and were disasters. For many, our public education system is broken. In addition, leadership is a major factor as well.

Education and Leadership

Many of the educators I work with in public school systems point to President Trump's appointee to the United States Secretary of Education, Betsy DeVos, as "a disaster". Lily Eskelsen Gracia, the National Education Association President (NEA) in 2016 stated, "Devos will be the first secretary of education with zero experience with public schools. She has never worked in a public school. She has never been a teacher, a school administrator, nor served on any public board of education. She didn't even attend public schools or send her children to public schools." (NEA 2018-2020). "Interestingly", DeVos has had extensive experience as the Republican National Committeewoman for Michigan from 1992 through 1997, served as chair of the Michigan Republican Party from 1996 through 2000, and then returned to serving as chair again in 2003.

In the book, *Good to Great*, Mr. Collins notes how nine out of ten Level 5 leaders came from within the company. Implicit in that empirical observation is a Level 5 leader has vast experience in many, if not all, aspects of an organization of which they are chosen to lead, and if this level of leaders do not (which is inevitable in a massive corporation), they are incredibly astute in securing the most qualified candidates for top level leadership positions. Utilizing the book *Good to Great*'s template, let us compare Betsy DeVos' previous experience before being appointed to the top educational position in the country, by President Trump, with the newly elected president of the NEA, Rebecca "Becky" Pringle.

Ms. Pringle started her career as a teacher in Philadelphia where she taught for thirty-one years, later she was employed as a middle school teacher in Harrisburg, Pennsylvania. She has been a part of the NEA for more than ten years, was elected to the union's vice president post, and now has been elected to the top position of the NEA, which is the largest union in the country. In addition, Ms. Pringle has served on the Board of Directors for the Pennsylvania State Education Association, as NEA's Executive Committee, and as the NEA treasurer. I realize this may be overkill on my part, however, Ms. Pringle also served on President Obama's Presidential Advisory Commission on Educational Excellence for African Americans, was part of the development team for the NEA's Policy Statement on Teacher Evaluation and Accountability, and has a record of being a consistent and outspoken advocate for championing fair and equal opportunities for disadvantaged youth.

I acknowledge this is sarcastic on my part, and I own it, but if only we could find someone who would have the depth of experience to be appointed to the post of our National Secretary of Education in our quest to provide equal educational opportunities to all. I support Ms. Pringle, and the NEA will be a force to make that quest a reality.

My father-in-law has also been on a lifelong quest to provide equal educational opportunities to all. I invite you to read Let's START with the CHILDREN, Journey to St. Ann's by Al Collela with Steven Lippincott. You may be thinking, well Al is his father-in-law, who he considers a father, he's married to Al's daughter, he could have a significant bias. Those concerns make perfect sense! However, I base my recommendation on knowing Al for over thirty-five years, and sometimes being in the trenches with him as well. I can say with absolute conviction that Al is a life-long educator who has dedicated much of his life to the micro and macro aspects of the educational process, and especially with helping those who start at a deficit because of the color of their skin, their socioeconomic status, and/or where they live. Al (Dr. Colella) is clear in the necessity of addressing the past in order to be able to move forward. If this sparks your curiosity, you may want to look at another book by: Al Colella, Ph.D. (and Joe Crowly) titled *Poverty & Despair vs. Education & Opportunity: Breaking Down the Barriers and Building Bridges*. Again, Mike's quote, "It makes the simple complex and the complex simple," amplifies Al and Joe's examination of our education system which clearly outlines the challenges and necessary long-term paradigm shifts to effect change. Can we agree the simple part is to start with the children?

Lastly, because IFS is not a psychological model alone, it can be adapted to other real life arenas. Joanna Curry-Sartori, LMFT is the executive director of the *Self Collaborative, Inc.* Together with her team of dedicated and experienced professionals, she has developed a curriculum for introducing the tenets of mindfulness, universal truths, and IFS for children in school systems. We can do it.

> **TO CONSIDER:** What are your ideas about education and the inequities in our country?

BIBLIOGRAPHY

Atkinson, Rita. Ruch, John. (1971). *Introduction to Psychology, Seventh Edition.* New York, New York: Harcourt Brace Jovanovich, Inc.

Bamberger, Jeanne. Brofsky, Howard. (1969, 1972). *The Art of Listening,:Developing Musical Perception.* New York, New York: Harper and Row Publishers.

Beck, Aaron. (1976). *Cognitive Therapy and the Emotional Disorders.* New York, New York: Penguin Group.

Beck, Aaron. Rush, A. John. Shaw, Brian. Emery, Gary. (1979). *Cognitive Therapy of Depression.* New York, New York: The Guilford Press.

Chung, Sau, Yeung (1976, 2000). *Practical Use of Tai Chi Chuan.* Boston, Massachusetts: Tai Chi Co, Chu Gin Soon.

Cleaver, Eldridge. (1968). *Soul on Ice.* New York, New York: Delta Trade Paperbacks.

Colella, Al. (2013). *Let's Start with the Children: Journey to St. Ann's.* Bloomington, IN: WestBow Press.

Colella, Albert. Crowley, Joseph. (2016). *Poverty and Despair versus Education and Opportunity: Breaking Down the Barriers and Building Bridges*: Stillwater River Publications.

Bibliography

Collins, Jim. (2001). *Good to Great*. New York, New York: HarperCollins Publishers Inc.

Cowen-Fletcher, Jane. (1994). *It Takes a Village*. New York, New York: Scholastic Inc.

Dana, Deb. (2018) *The Polyvagal Theory in Therapy: ENGAGING THE RHYTHM OF REGULATION*.

De Becker, Gavin. (1997). *The Gift of Fear, and Other Survival Signals that Protect Us From Violence*. New York, New York: Dell Publishing.

De Becker, Gavin. Taylor, Tom. Marquart, Jeff. (2008). *Just 2 Seconds: Using Time and Space to Defeat Assassins and other Adversaries*. Studio City, California: The Gavin De Becker Center.

De Becker, Gavin. (1999) *Protecting the Gift: Keeping Children and Teenagers Safe (and Parents Sane)*. Dell Publishing.

Farber, I. Harlow, Harry. Jolyon West, Louis. (1957). *Brainwashing, Conditioning, and DDD (Debility, Dependency and Dread. Sociomentry*, (1957) Volume 20.

Figley, Charles. (1985). *Trauma and its Wake: The Study and Treatment of Post-Traumatic Stress Disorder*. New York, New York: Brunner/Mazel Inc.

Fisher, Robert. Ury, William. Patton, Bruce. (1991, 2001) *Getting to YES: Negotiating Agreement Without Giving In*. Penguin Group.

Fisher, Roger. Ury, William. Patton, Bruce. (2011). *Getting to Yes: Negotiating Agreement without Giving In*. New York, New York: Penguin Group.

Goleman, Daniel. (1995). *Emotional Intelligence*. New York, New York: Bantam Dell.

Goulding, Regina. Schwartz, Richard. (1995). *The Mosaic Mind: Empowering the Tormented Selves of Child Abuse Survivors.* New York, New York: W. W. Norton and Company.

Grossman, Dave, Lt. Col. (1995) *On Killing: The Psychological Cost of Learning to Kill in War and Society.* Little, Brown and Company.

Grossman, Dave, Lt. Col. and DeGaetano, Gloria. (1999) *Stop Teaching our Kids to Kill. A Call to Action Against TV, Movie & Video Game Violence.* Crown Publishers, NY.

Hackworth, David, H. Colonel, and Sherman, Julie. (1989) *About Face.* Simon and Schuster.

Herman, Judith. (1992). *Trauma and Recovery: The aftermath of violence—from domestic abuse to political terror.* New York, New York: BasicBooks.

Hill Jr, Thomas. Zweig, Arnulf. (2002). *Kant: Groundwork for the Metaphysics of Morals.* New York: Oxford University Press Inc.

James, Beverly. (1994). *Handbook for Treatment of Attachment-Trauma Problems in Children.* New York, New York: Lexington Books.

Karen, Robert (1992). *Shame.* The Atlantic Monthly, February.

Karen, Robert. (1992). *Shame.* The Atlantic Monthly.

McCann, Lisa. Pearlman, Laurie. (1990). *Psychological Trauma and the Adult Survivor, Theory, Therapy, and Transformation.* New York, New York: Brunner/Mazel Inc.

Miller, William. Rollnick, Stephen. (1991). *Motivational Interviewing: Preparing People to Change Addictive Behavior.* New York, New York: The Guilford Press.

Bibliography

Morris, William. (1969). *The American Heritage Onary of the English Language*. New York, New York: American Heritage Publishing Co Inc, Houghton Mifflin Company.

Nathanson, Donald. (1992). *Shame and Pride*. New York, New York: W.W. Norton and Company.

National Association of Social Workers. (1996). *Code of Ethics*. Washington, DC: NASW Delegate Assembly.

National Association of Social Workers. (2017). *Code of Ethics*. Washington, DC: NASW Delegate Assembly.

Navarro, Joe. Karlins, Marvin. (2008). *What Every Body is Saying*. New York, New York: Harper-Collins Publishers.

Obama, Michelle. (2018) *Becoming*. Crown Publishing Group, a division of Penguin Random House, LLC.

O'Brien, Tim. (1990). *The Things They Carried*. New York, New York: Houghton Mifflin Harcourt Publishing Company.

Porges, Stephen. (2011). *The Polyvagal Theory: Neurophysiological Foundations of Emotions, Attachment, Communication, and Self-Regulation*. Norton books.

Schwartz, Richard. (2001). *Introduction to the Internal Family Systems Model*. Oak Park, Illinois: Trailheads Publications.

Schwartz, Richard. (2001). *Introduction to the Internal Family Systems Model*. Oak Park, Illinois: Trailheads Publications.

Schwartz, Richard. Falconer, Robert (2017). *Many Minds One Self: Evidence for a Radical Shift in Paradigm*. Oak Park, Illinois: Trailheads Publications.

Schwartz, Richard. Sweezy, Martha. (2020). *Internal Family Systems Therapy, Second Edition.* New York, New York: The Guilford Press.

Schwartz, Richard., Goulding, Regina. (1995). *The Mosaic Mind.* New York, New York: W.W. Norton and Company.

Shapiro, Francine. (2001). *Eye Movement Desensitization and Reprocessing: Basic Principles, Protocols, and Procedures.* New York, New York: The Guilford Press.

Sweezy, Martha. Ziskind, Ellen. (2017) *IFS: Innovations and Elaborations in Internal Family Systems Therapy.* New York, New York: Routledge.

Timerman, Jacobo. (1988). *Prisoner without a Name, Cell without a Number.* New York: Random House Inc.

Towles, Amor. (2016). *A Gentleman in Moscow.* London, UK: Windmill Books.

Ury, William. (1991, 1993, 2007). *Getting Past NO: Negotiating in Difficult Situations.* Bantam Books. (Director of the Global Negotiation Project at Harvard University)

Van der Kolk, Bessel A. (2014). *The Body Keeps the Score, Brain: Mind, and Body in the Healing of Trauma.* New York, New York: Penguin Group.

Van der Kolk, Bessel. (1987). *Psychological Trauma.* Washington, DC: American Psychiatric Press, Inc.

Ward, Geoffrey C. and Burns, Ken. (2017) *The Vietnam War: An Intimate History.* Alfred A Knopf, New York.

Webster. (1986). *Webster's Ninth New Collegiate Dictionary.* Springfield, Massachusetts: Merriam-Webster Inc.

Williams, Hywel. (2009). *Great Speeches of Our Time*. London: Quercus Publishing Plc.

Windham, Ryder. (2007). *Star Wars, Jedi versus Sith: The Essential Guide to the Force.* Random House, Inc: Del Rey Books.

Yang, Chengfu. (2005). Swaim, Louis. *The Essence and Applications of Taijiquan.* Berkeley, California: Blue Snake Books.

Young, Deran. (2018). *Black Therapist Rock: A Glimpse Through the Eyes of Experts.*

PHOTOGRAPHY CREDITS

Photos of *Practical Use of Tai Chi Chuan* courtesy of Master Vincent Chu, Gin Soon Tai Chi Federation. Master Gin Soon was the second disciple of Yeung Sau Chung.

Bożanowski, Kuba. "Steve Smith on Drum, with Vital Information, 18th Eventus DrumFest Opole 2009." *Wikimedia Commons,* The Wikimedia Project, Opole, Poland, 29 Apr. 2013, commons.wikimedia.org/wiki/File:Steve_Smith_on_drum,_with_Vital_Information,_18th_Eventus_DrumFest_Opole_2009.jpg. No changes were made.

Fraser MacPherson estate c/o Guy MacPherson. "Louie Bellson." *Wikimedia Commons,* The Wikimedia Project, 21 Apr. 2008, commons.wikimedia.org/wiki/File:Louis_Bellson.jpg. No changes were made.

Spürk, Paul. "Buddy Rich." *Wikimedia Commons,* The Wikimedia Project, Cologne, Germany, 1 Mar. 2008, commons.wikimedia.org/wiki/File:Buddyrich.jpg. No changes were made.